vs

Todd McFarlane

Daniel Best

The World vs Todd McFarlane by Daniel Best.

Published by Blaq Books
PO Box 3315
Norwood, South Australia, 5067
Australia

Cover by Darren Close

Portions of this work originally appeared on the blog 20th Century Danny Boy

(http://ohdannyboy.blogspot.com)

ISBN: 9781796687002

BLAQ BOOKS

CONTENTS

NEIL
GAIMAN &
TODD
McFARLANE

A BRIEF NOTE ON SOURCES

The bulk of his manuscript has been sourced directly from court documents including, but not limited to, affidavits, depositions, trial transcripts and settlements, along with period and new interviews, newspaper articles and more.

By their very nature, court documents are often contradictory and can lead to errors, which is why the author has not selected to tell one side of the story only.

The author is more than willing to make changes to future editions if any factual errors can be found. Simply email him at snoopy967@gmail.com.

Cast of Characters

Al Simmons. College friend and baseball team-mate of Todd McFarlane. McFarlane named *Spawn*'s alter ego after Simmons.

Alan Davis. Writer/Artist. The second main artist on *Marvelman/Miracleman.*

Alan Moore. Writer. Wrote *Marvelman* for *Warrior* and the continued to write *Miracleman* for Eclipse. Also wrote *Spawn* #8 for McFarlane, along with the *Violator* and *Spawn: Bloodfeud* mini-series.

Allan Inglis. Joined TMP International in August of 1996. Was the CFO of Todd McFarlane Productions International (TMPI) until June of 2001.

Brian Holguin. Writer of *Spawn: The Dark Ages.*

Cat Yronwode. Former EIC at Eclipse Comics. Former wife of Dean Mullaney.

Dean Mullaney. Co-Owner of Eclipse Comics. Former husband of Cat Yronwode.

Erik Larsen. Co-founder of Image Comics. Writer, artist and creator of *Savage Dragon* for Image. Followed McFarlane as the artist on both *The Amazing Spider-Man* and *Spider-Man*.

Gareb Shamus. Former founder and EIC of *Wizard*. One-time close friend of Todd McFarlane. Co-defendant in the Tony Twist case.

Jan Mullaney. Co-Owner of Eclipse comics. Handled payments. At times in brown paper bags.

Larry Marder. Writer, artist and creator of *Beanworld*. Worked at both Eclipse Comics and Image Comics. President of Todd McFarlane Productions. Sits on, and is Vice President of, the board of directors of Todd McFarlane's companies.

Mark Buckingham. Artist. Worked with Gaiman on *Miracleman: The Golden Age*.

Neil Gaiman. Writer. Most famous for his run on *Sandman* for DC Comics. Wrote issue #9 of *Spawn*. Created *Angela* for McFarlane's *Spawn*. Took over the writing chores and ownership of *Miracleman*.

Rob Liefeld. Co-founder of Image Comics. Writer, artist and creator of *Youngblood, Deadpool, X-Force, Cable* and many more. Had a brutal falling out with McFarlane in 1996 resulting in Liefeld leaving Image.

Terry Fitzgerald. Former President and COO of McFarlane Entertainment. One of Todd's oldest friends; helped form TMP with McFarlane. McFarlane named a major character in *Spawn* after Fitzgerald.

Todd McFarlane. Artist, writer, businessman, ice hockey team and baseball owner. Creator and publisher of Spawn. Part owner of Image Comics.

Tony Twist. Ice hockey player. Known as a 'goon'.

Foreword

In this book Daniel Best holds up for our scrutiny the inner workings—the gory guts, if you will—of Todd McFarlane's numerous legal clashes. And those gory guts are glorious indeed.

I'm not completely sure how long I've known Daniel, but I know how we first got in touch. I had seriously started to write my own recent book, *Poisoned Chalice*, about *Marvelman* and *Miracleman*, albeit very slowly, back in 2010. As it got closer to the present time, I was relying more and more on the Internet, and on Google, to help with the research. Sometime in or before March 2012 I must have put in right combination of words that brought me to one of his posts on the legal shenanigans relating to Neil Gaiman and Todd McFarlane, because I linked to a post on his 20th Century Danny Boy blog on the 19th of March, which was followed by an exchange of emails between us the following day, beginning a correspondence and a friendship that has continued to this day.

One of the reasons I linked to his work back then, and am delighted to be able to write this introduction now, is because it's so good. Really. Daniel's work is, as far as I'm concerned, the gold standard in how to do your research. I have learnt a lot from his research, things I'd never have found out on my own, and it's certainly the case that my own work would be the lesser without having his work to build upon. I hope that I am not being presumptuous in saying that this book and my own book are essentially companion volumes to one another. Certainly we have both become fascinated with specific aspects of much bigger pictures, and have both chosen to take our own paths, and plough our own furrows, in our own ways, and have hopefully both added a little light to a complex and, for us, a fascinating still ongoing situation.

Where Daniel succeeds, and I did not, is in being kind about McFarlane and his actions. But he's right, and I'm wrong. The older I get, the more I believe in redemption, and giving even the worst of us another chance. It is obvious that he has no intention of standing in judgement on his subject, in the very best legal way.

He's found the evidence and presented it in an impartial manner. Make up your own mind. But first, read the book!

Pádraig Ó Méalóid

Pádraig Ó Méalóid is the author of Poisoned Chalice, The Extremely Long and Incredibly Complex Story of Marvelman (and Miracleman)

Introduction

Each generation of comic books seems to throw up at least one person who manages to polarize the entire medium. Be it Stan Lee, John Byrne, Frank Miller, Jim Shooter, Alan Moore, Jim Steranko, Neal Adams or, these days, Ethan Van Sciver, creators have often been either loved or hated by the masses for any number of reasons. They're either looked upon as credit stealing hogs (Lee and, to a lesser extent, Shooter), having controversial opinions that go against popular views (Byrne and Van Sciver) or just plain nuts (Miller).

It's a rare creator who gains the respect of the entire industry, even the seemingly untouchable greats, including Jack Kirby and Stan Lee, without their critics.

When it comes to dividing an entire industry, there's one artist who stands above all others.

Todd Dean Mark McFarlane.

There are those who consider Todd McFarlane to be the most exciting artist to emerge from the post *Watchmen* era. Equally there are those who consider McFarlane to be the single most destructive force for the same period.

McFarlane, depending on who you talk to, revolutionized the industry. He modernized the field with his art and single handedly dragged the entire comic book industry into a new age. He became one of the richest creators and, instead of just talking about the injustices of Work-For-Hire, left Marvel Comics at the height of his popularity to spearhead the formation of Image Comics, where he's remained to this day.

On the other hand, Todd McFarlane is the worst thing to happen to comic books since Fredric Wertham. His art was all flash and no substance. His poses were unrealistic. He spawned what seemed to be an endless number of imitators, most of whom didn't have an ounce of his abilities. He stole characters away from the likes of Neil Gaiman – a capital offence for many. He's brash, open, opinionated, abrasive and often abusive. In short, he's a prick. Plus, he couldn't write to save his life.

When it comes to Todd McFarlane there are a few things that are well worth remembering. Yes, he became insanely rich, but he did manage to spread that wealth around, when it suited him. Those who worked for Todd McFarlane's companies got paid, and paid well at that. He looked after those he brought with him, and he was loyal to those who were loyal to him.

McFarlane appears to love his fans and will go out of his way to accommodate them at conventions, often sitting for hours on end signing items and answering questions.

McFarlane is known for his marathon signing sessions and, if called away from his table at a convention, will always put a note up telling people when he will be returning.

Where some creators have a list of items that they will not sign, either officially or unofficially, McFarlane appears to not overly care. He'll sign a copy of *Spider-Man* #300 as happily as he will a copy of *Spawn* #1. The only two comics that McFarlane has openly said he will not sign are variant covers – the retailer only 'Thank You' *Spawn* #1 and the recent *Venom* #1 variant issued by Marvel Comics.

He even co-signed an issue of *Spawn* #9 immediately after losing the first Neil Gaiman case. The other person who signed it, while McFarlane held it?

Neil Richard MacKinnon Gaiman.

While McFarlane is very generous to those he likes, he is as equally as savage to his foes. He does not tolerate fools lightly and, considering his status in the industry, he doesn't need to.

It'd be hard to find anyone interested in comic books and their history who hasn't heard of Todd McFarlane's legal woes, but very few outside of McFarlane's immediate circle know just how many legal fights he was facing as the 1990s closed.

Virtually all of McFarlane's court cases came down to three decisions, made by him alone.

The first was to name a mobster in his *Spawn* comic after a hockey player, Tony Twist.

The second was to hire Neil Gaiman to write a single issue of *Spawn.*

The third came when he decided to buy all the remaining assets from Eclipse Comics at their bankruptcy sale.

Everything else, as you'll see, always comes back to one of those three core choices.

His bankruptcy came because of the Twist trial.

Gaiman taking him to court for ownership and payment of work comes down to McFarlane hiring him to write *Spawn #9.*

His losing of the *Miracleman* brand would never have happened if he hadn't thought that he had bought it in the first place.

Never mind the many instances of broken promises and lies, none of it would have happened but for the three core choices.

The Tony Twist trial was the beginning of a long, long period of uncertainty for Todd McFarlane and very nearly brought down the empire that he'd worked so hard to build.

At its worst point, McFarlane was fighting to save his companies, to keep his characters and simply to survive. He was facing battles from several fronts, from people he did not previously personally know in the form of Tony Twist, to those whom he'd collaborated with, in the form of Neil Gaiman and also in bankruptcy courts.

Clearly the fight that cost him the most, in purely financial terms, was that brought against him by Tony Twist. It would take years, and millions of dollars, to finally resolve. But the fight that potentially hurt him the most, both personally and professionally, was the one brought by Gaiman, as it gave the impression that McFarlane had appropriated characters created by Gaiman without proper accounting, permission or payments. This, to the comic book industry at large, appeared to show McFarlane as being no better than the corporations that he'd spent years rallying against – Marvel and DC Comics.

It would take the better part of two decades before McFarlane would emerge free and clear from these fights. He came out of it battered, bruised, facing charges of hypocrisy and a serious hit to his reputation, but he wasn't totally beaten. Despite those who wished to see McFarlane fall completely from grace, he emerged relatively intact.

For those observing from the outside, McFarlane sailed through these years with a breeze. He rarely exhibited any public display of discomfort about the many court cases. But it was far from smooth sailing for Todd McFarlane.

This book will show the extent of McFarlane's legal woes while both confirming and debunking a lot of the myths and stories that have sprung up since Tony Twist first decided to sue. Not only will you read about Todd McFarlane, but you'll also read about others connected with McFarlane, including Eclipse Comics, Tony Twist, Neil Gaiman, Image Comics, Marvel Comics and many more.

McFarlane Pre-Image

> "I was collecting bubble gum cards and other things. It was just part of collecting. Once I got those (comic books) - I think I got about five that day - the floodgate went ptooosh! I became just psycho about comics after that.[1]" – Todd McFarlane.

Todd McFarlane was born in Calgary, Canada, on 16 March 1961.

"I attended Spokane Falls Community College starting in, I think, the beginning of 1980, spent about a year and a half there and then transferred over to Eastern Washington University and stayed there until graduation in 1984," recalled McFarlane. "Graduation about May of '84, started working for Marvel Comics, sort of a subdivision called Epic Comics, had a short stint, probably for four or five months; and then from there jumped over to DC.[2]"

Breaking into comics wasn't as easy for McFarlane as people might imagine. "It was rough, and I was keeping track of everything," he said in 1999. "I had a little chart: I sent out like 750 packages and half of them got no responses and half of them got rejections. My wife was cleaning out the closet the other day and came across a bag of rejection letters. I used to carry them (around), and I'd pour them on the table, moaning, 'I sent out two packages, and I don't have a job and I'm discouraged.' I used to literally have my bag full, and I'd just go pkeeewwwf! I somehow made it. You've got to persevere, right? You're not going to get a job your first two cracks at it.[3]"

McFarlane expanded upon his early years in his 2002 deposition. "I was the penciler on a back-up series for a comic titled Steve Engelhart's *Coyote*. Although I was only doing a backup, the book got cancelled so essentially I had no work. And so I went back to somebody I'd met and sent and corresponded with earlier and I was able to pick up another job. Initially it was a couple of what we call fill in issues, which are sort of temp jobs to get you through from month to month, but it turned into a permanent job, which was the penciler on a book titled *Infinity, Incorporated*, as a free-lancer for about three years.

"Everybody is sort of looking out for their career and I'd been on the book for three years and I was looking. It was a team. It may seem silly, but it was a team book which meant it had a lot of characters in it and it can get very arduous drawing a lot of different people. So I was looking to see if I could grab a job that was sort of more focused on a headline character than doing twenty guys in a book. About '88; went back to Marvel. I think I did a couple fill ins for them just to sort of show them I can meet a deadline and then they gave me the *Incredible Hulk* to pencil.[4]"

His early days, penciling *Coyote* (Epic Comics, a Marvel Comics imprint) and *Infinity Inc.* (DC Comics) allowed him time, and space, to develop a unique style of art, one which borrowed from many sources; from John Byrne, Frank Miller, Michael Golden, Walter Simonson, Ross Andru and Steve Ditko. Some of these influences were clear, some were influences by osmosis. McFarlane's art was big and splashy, he drew fine lines and lots of them, hyper detailed with figures placed in poses that were anatomically impossible.

McFarlane was undisciplined and hard to edit. "I'm uncoachable," he said in 1993, at the height of his fame. "And that's the thing that you can understand, like am I an idiot that I got peers that hate me 'cause they think that I am a whatever, some weird, wacked out guy, ah yeah, but I'm the same with my wife, so it's like, you know she seems to love me for it. I'm the same with everything. So don't take it personally that I didn't listen to every order I got at Marvel because I don't listen to practically... I'm uncoachable. My wife has known that since I was playing baseball, that I'm uncoachable. When I set my mind I don't listen to nobody, because then, if it doesn't work out and I crash and burn, then I can live with it, you know? I can live with failure as long as I'm the one that steered the failure.[5]"

In his early days, McFarlane was lucky enough to be paired with the likes of Roy Thomas (*Infinity Inc.*) which helped him learn the craft of pacing and storytelling. McFarlane was the perfect artist for superhero comic books; his exaggerations and over the top styling suited the medium down to the ground.

But this style didn't happen overnight, it would take years to develop and perfect. In fact, his early work on *Infinity Inc.* bore very little resemblance to what was to come. To be frank, his early work was pedestrian and ordinary, yet serviceable, and McFarlane knew it.

"As an artist, you always feel lucky to have a job," McFarlane said in 2009. "It's like any day you are working, you feel like you have won the lotto. I think I'm a good example of perseverance. When I finally broke in I was very mediocre. I was below average when I started my first job. But they put me to work doing it for eight hours a day. When you do something every day for that long, you get better and better.[6]"

McFarlane soon became schooled in the politics of how the comic book industry worked. "So you start climbing the ladder in promotions and comic books," he said. "The companies don't give you money - but they give you characters. They knew which character was the favorite for each guy. So when (an artist) would come in there, (the editors) would say, 'OK, his favorite's Green Lantern.' And when the artist would ask for more money, (the editors) would say, 'Can't do it. But if you keep your nose straight, we've got the Green Lantern annual coming, and we haven't picked the team yet, and there's a chance...' And the (artist) would go floating out the door. He never did do the Green Lantern, and he didn't get a raise.[7]"

McFarlane really hit his straps as the 1980s drew to a close. First it was a run on *The Hulk*, where, paired with writer Peter David, he helped bring the book back to popularity and, with his now iconic cover art for issue 340, created an instant collectable. Not that McFarlane was being handed a premier book. At the time he was given the art chores on a book that was considered to be just another Marvel comic, and, aside from a short-lived run by writer/artist John Byrne, the title wasn't generating much in the way of sales.

Peter David recalled his first introduction to McFarlane's art... After being asked to write the title by editor Bob Harras, Harras "...also asked if I wouldn't mind working with this artist they had on the book, Todd McFarlane. His art was seriously flawed, so much so that at least one other writer had refused to work with him, but Bob saw something there and felt he had potential. He was reluctant to take him off the book to make room for me. I don't know for sure that Bob would have fired him off the book to accommodate me, but I didn't want to take the chance of costing someone else his gig. I looked at McFarlane's art pages for the last Al Milgrom written issue, and it was kind of lousy, but I'd seen worse - hell, I'd worked with worse - and I agreed with Bob... there did seem to be potential there. So I shrugged and said, 'Sure, I can work with him.'

"Absolutely no one at Marvel cared what I was doing on the book. *Incredible Hulk* didn't even register on anyone's editorial scope. It was sufficiently low end, I guess, to avoid hassle I did what I could creatively to get the series noticed by the fans, and also did everything I could to accommodate the artist. Todd wanted to draw big machines and robots, so I kept putting in scenes that called for that. Todd wanted to draw Wolverine and I moved heaven and earth–including a good deal of negotiation with the X-office, who really didn't want to loan him out–to use him for an issue (#340). Todd gave me the cover for that issue, the one piece of McFarlane art I own.[8]"

Following that were a three issue fill in run on *Detective Comics*, where he took over the art chores for Mike Barr's *Year Two* storyline from Alan Davis and Paul Neary.

"Alan Davis drew a picture of Batman on the covers of one of the *Detective Comics* with a gun," remembers Neary. "They came back and said that the gun had been redesigned again, in another magazine. In *Batman: Year One* they had the origin of Batman, how Batman came to be and David Mazzuchelli had redrawn the scene where Batman's dad was shot. He had redrawn that and they used this bloody great semi-automatic Mauser, instead of a little sort of hand gun. Alan thought this was ridiculous and absolutely crazy, because he had drawn Batman on the cover with the little gun and they redrew it. Dick Giordano called up and said he was sorry; he was going to have to redraw it. According to Alan, it didn't work as a cover anymore and that was the end of it.[9]"

DC Comics instantly placed McFarlane on the book to finish the storyline, which he did. Then came *Invasion*, a title which enabled him to draw virtually every single DC Comics character.

"When I was doing the *Hulk* I was building speed and so I was then capable of doing more than one book a month, and so I'd picked up the odd job," said McFarlane. "When I left DC, I told a couple of people I'll come back and do some *Batman* and the opportunity came up to do some *Batman*. It was only temporary, three months. I did that, and once that job ended, I'm down to one book. I can actually do two books. And so I went looking for another job and I ended up getting the *Amazing Spider-Man*.[10]"

The Amazing Spider-Artist

The one single character that Todd McFarlane is known for, even more so than *Spawn*, is the *Amazing Spider-Man*. Everything he does is in the shadow of his work on the character, which is comprised of twenty eight issues of *The Amazing Spider-Man*[1] and fifteen issues of the adjective less *Spider-Man*[2].

Created by Steve Ditko and Stan Lee in 1962, and long considered to be one of the flagship titles for Marvel Comics, *The Amazing Spider-Man* had seen a revolving door of artists for the previous years, including Alan Kupperberg, Erik Larsen, Paul Ryan, Cyndi Martin, Mike Zeck, Alex Saviuk, Tom Morgan, Ron Frenz, John Romita Sr, John Romita Jr and Rick Leonardi amongst others.

Adding to the mix of artist were the two other *Spider-Man* titles, *Web of Spider-Man* and *Spectacular Spider-Man* where artists such as Sal Buscema, Steve Geiger, Marc Silvestri, Larry Lieber, Greg LaRoq, Jim Fern, Jim Mooney, Frank Miller, Del Barras, Rich Buckler, Al Milgrom, John Byrne, Bob McLeod and others had worked.

From 1980 to 1988 Spider-Man had been drawn by dozens of artists, most with their own unique style, with the result being that the character no longer had the singular, consistent look that it did in the 1960s and 1970s when John Romita

Sr oversaw the line. Even Editor-In-Chief, Jim Shooter, had thrown his hand into the mix in the mid-80s by providing layouts for three issues of *Spectacular Spider-Man* with the view of showing others how Marvel wanted the character drawn. The irony was that Shooter was an editor and writer. Although he could draw, his art was stilted and stiff.

Occasionally Romita himself would pencil or ink and issue, along with Jim Mooney, who had begun work at Marvel in the mid-60s[3]. Mike Esposito, who had inked Romita's first ever *Spider-Man* stories in the '60s, would ink some issues. John Romita Jr, who's early style mirrored his famous father closely, would also pencil the character.

The primary hold over from the 1960s was the overall look of the main cast of the books. Every artist was instructed to draw Mary Jane – Peter Parker's love interest and later wife – to look the same as John Romita's original vision from *Amazing Spider-Man* #43 (December 1966). Those who attempted to do otherwise soon found their art whited out and a John Romita drawn head placed over the top. But what was fashionable and worked in 1966, didn't quite translate to 1986.

Things weren't helped by editorial influence. Mike Esposito, while inking Sal Buscema on the pages of *Spectacular Spider-Man,* was instructed to 'rough' the inking, with the view of making the pencils look scratchy. Buscema, on the other hand, was told that Esposito was slacking off and deliberately roughing his pencils up[4]. The end result wasn't pleasing to the readers.

In short, *Spider-Man,* while not stale by an stretch of the imagination, was prime for an artistic shake-up.

McFarlane began his run with issue 298, and, paired with writer David Michelinie and inker Bob McLeod, helped bring that title back into flagship status for Marvel, with the duo creating one of the most enduring villains of the modern era in the form of *Venom.*

"It seems weird, but Spider-Man was really in a disarray when I got there," he said in 1999. "They had the three books - Amazing, *Spectacular…*, *Web of…* - and, for whatever reason, they were changing the creative team over and over and over and over. I just happened to really be in the right place at the right time. I went over to Marvel looking for another job, and literally stuck my head in all the editors' offices. That's how you get jobs. 'Oh, yeah, so-and-so just quit last week. You want to do the book?' You don't really push people off books. It just happens to be people leaving or deadlines or whatever. My very first regular job I got was because someone, like, died. You need those breaks. The only thing that everyone did say was, 'Todd, don't go in the Spider-Man office. You don't want to work in the Spider-Man office.' I was like, 'Oh, cool. I'm going in the Spider-Man office.' They ended up offering me *Amazing Spider-Man*, which to me was like the granddaddy."[5]

Realizing that he might not be there long, McFarlane hit the ground running and began to change the overall look of the book. "Some of the stuff I'm doing just hasn't been updated since the '60s," he said. "The reason It looks so much different and some of the people are having heart attack over It, is that it hasn't been updated for 20 years. If they had been updating it every five years, it wouldn't have been such a big deal.[6]"

He turned Mary-Jane Watson from the 1966 straight haired, John Romita style beauty, into his own version of a super model, complete with big, curly hair and a voluptuous figure. "They're telling me her occupation is a three-quarter of a million dollar a year model a la Cheryl Tiegs," he explained. "And I'm saying Cheryl Tiegs doesn't walk around with a hippie hairdo and wear K-Mart clothing. So I went through Vogue and starting drawing her with a '90s look.[7]"

McFarlane didn't settle with updating Mary Jane and Spider-Man. He moved his eye towards updating Peter Parker, turning him from a nerdish type into an urbane, muscular young man with a modern haircut. Other characters in the book, both main and supporting, along with the rouge's gallery, also found themselves 'McFarlaneized' as he slowly made the book his own.

"People say I have some of Steve Ditko's original feeling," he said, "but when I analyzed it, my stuff isn't that close to his. I'm like thousands of others. I had the perception of what he did. He made the eyes bigger and I make eyes bigger. He put on a lot of webbing and a lot of black in Spider-Man's costumes. But the actual style isn't that close. Every five years, there seems to be a different style that sells to kids. It's sort of like clothing. You update and refine them.

"Ditko did about the first 40 issues[8], then Romita took over and worked on it twice as long. Romita's Spider-Man is the one you see on lunch boxes and beach towels. It's the definitive classic Spider-Man. Romita made as big a mark as Ditko did. He had done romance comics, and with Spider-Man everything had a soft look. All the girls were pretty and the men were handsome, where with Ditko, everybody wasn't perfect.[9]"

Even something as mundane and simplistic as Spider-Man's trademark web-line was altered forever by McFarlane, changing from a straight line into something resembling spaghetti.

"The webbing idea came from an old black-and-white piece," McFarlane said. "Years ago you guys used to put out these black-and-white portfolios, around 1980 or something like that, and there was one piece that was the *Defenders* by Mike Golden, and for whatever reason he had *Spider-Man* in it. He did this great *Spider-Man* with this funky webbing, and I kept that piece out of all the pieces. And I go, 'If I ever turn into a comic-book pro, and if I ever work for Marvel Comics, and if I ever get to do *Spider-Man*, I'm going to do webbing like that!' And this was in 1980, so I was just a baby collecting comic books. Nineteen years of age and it just kind of hit me like a bolt, so when I finally got my chance I go, 'Yeah, it's time to dig out that drawing that Mike Golden did and do the spaghetti webbing!' He had to do it straight, it was my idea to make it kind of like a cowboy guy; but the ultimate origin of the spaghetti webbing, the honors go to Mike Golden.[10]"

McFarlane's changes didn't happen as neatly or quietly as even he might have thought. There were those within the Marvel system who felt that McFarlane, despite his popularity, still couldn't draw properly. However, Romita never redrew the heads of Mary Jane to reflect his own vision, and McFarlane took this as an acceptance of his work. This was far from the truth. In fact Romita found that he couldn't redraw the heads on McFarlane's work without it looking too obvious.

One Marvel staffer at the time, when asked about McFarlane's art was brutal in his assessment. "I don't think Romita tried to redraw the heads," the author was told, "because it would have looked too jarring to have a well-drawn head on an atrociously drawn body. McFarlane's early figures barely looked human, much less like the established characters. But his art was dynamic and 'new' and he sold comics. So they left him alone.[11]"

Ironically McFarlane's friend and Image Comics co-founder, Rob Liefeld, was also having a similar issue, often providing the barest of detail in his pencils. "They were actually kind of sketchy and if I remember right one of the issues was done from little layouts, which meant they had to be photocopied," inker Joe Rubinstein remembered. "He did them like miniatures. Then they were photocopied up to 11" x 17"- the size of a comic book like seven pages, traced and then I inked them, so that meant an awful lot of energy was lost in the process.[12]"

In Liefeld's case, Romita did step in to redraw heads to keep them within the Marvel style, raising the ire of Liefeld. This happened with the cover art to *The New Mutants* #85 when Romita re-drew the face of Odin, with the finished pencils inked by McFarlane. As expected, the style of John Romita clashed with those of Liefeld and McFarlane with Odin's face standing out like the proverbial sore thumb.

A study of McFarlane's pencils, both from his time on *The Hulk* and *The Amazing Spider-Man* bear the theory of McFarlane's failings out. In virtually all cases, his pencils are rough and unfinished. This meant the inker assigned to the issue had to do a lot of finishing on his work. McFarlane's true strength as an artist lay in his inks and finishes; he was never as good an artist as he was when he inked his own work, or inked the work of others. He finally took over the full art duties on *The Amazing Spider-Man* with the landmark 300th issue and began to fully weave his own style.

Some liked McFarlane's style, some didn't. One who did was a man who'd later work with McFarlane, and destined to become a partner at Image Comics, *Walking Dead* creator Robert Kirkman. "Todd mastered something in a way that few have - favoring things that look cool over things that look correct. I love how he drew Spider-Man's thighs. They're bent in ways that a thigh doesn't, because there's a femur in there. But if you zoom out and look at how it's moving, it's the most dynamic thing. Now you see Spider-Man in movies being all twisted and looking cool, and that was achieved by not being beholden to reality.[13]"

Not everyone was as enthusiastic about McFarlane's style as others. Fantagraphics founder and editor of *The Comics Journal,* Gary Growth, remains a staunch critic. "He doesn't have any authentic virtues as a visual stylist. His work is so over embellished that it disguised the fact that the composition is chaotic and cluttered to the point of being almost unreadable. He never really learned the craft of comics - he just faked it really well.[14]"

Ultimately it didn't matter what the critics or even his own peers thought or said.

The true test of success in the comic book industry has always been sales figures. Sales spoke volumes and the sales for McFarlane's *Spider-Man* increased to the point where it was Marvel's number one selling book. Soon it would be McFarlane's rendition of Spider-Man on towels, lunchboxes, posters and shirts, rather than Romita or Ditko's.

McFarlane was a hot artist, instead of being told to draw Mary Jane, Peter Parker and the cast like Romita, artists assigned to the *Spider-Man* lines were being told to draw like McFarlane[15]. Some tried, and failed, others merely ignored the orders and went on their own ways. One thing that McFarlane proved was that the books needed regular creative teams, thus Alex Saviuk was assigned *Web of Spider-Man* and Sal Buscema *Spectacular Spider-Man.* The concessions each artist gave to McFarlane were the use of the 'spaghetti' webbing and the updated looks for both Peter Parker and Mary Jane Watson.

The Amazing Spider-Man was a monthly book, but it soon became bi-weekly, to cash in on McFarlane's popularity. Realizing he needed assistance to produce the book, he put out a call for a full-time assistant. It was then that McFarlane would meet, and hire, Terry Fitzgerald, who would remain by McFarlane's side, serving as a Man Friday, from 1988 onwards.

"Back in early 1988," Fitzgerald would later recall, "Todd had come down to the local high school of this shithole little town we lived in called Duncan. He was trying to get someone out of the art class to do some blacks and assisting. I'd been out of school for two years at that point. I was in college then getting a Bachelor of Science. I was going to become a pharmacist. My girlfriend I was seeing at the time was in one of these art classes. She said this guy is supposed to be the hottest comic-book artist, blah, blah, blah. He was looking for someone to come work for him. This was on a Friday. He was giving an interview on the following Monday. Considering she didn't have a car, I had to drive her. I thought, since she was doing it, I might as well, too. So, the whole weekend, we did up samples and went over there. In typical Todd fashion, "I'll have you out by seven:' I think it was midnight before I got out of there. We were the last ones out. He said, whoever he picked he'd phone tomorrow night at seven. So, she and I sat by the phone at seven. 7:30 came... eight. Nothing. Around 9:30 or 10:00, I called my girlfriend. "Did you hear anything?" "No:' I told her to go to school tomorrow and find out who it was. I was curious as to who Todd picked. It was about 11:30. We were all sleeping in the house. The phone rings. I was living at home, and my mom comes screaming down the hallway: "Hey, Terry, one of your bloody friends for ya!" Todd: "Yeah, uh, can you come in to work around nine tomorrow?" That's how this whole tumultuous relationship began.

“He was a complete wild man. I spent the first two weeks working for him laughing. Everything that came out of his mouth was funny to me. "Can you pass me the eraser?" It was the goofiest thing. Anybody who knows Todd knows he's funny, even unintentionally. He's good with jokes. We used to listen to this Christian program on AM radio which is funny because Todd is an atheist. I'd listen to it and hear Todd go, "Oh, shit! That's absolutely #$%&* bullshit:' He'd banter back and forth with this guy on the radio. It was pretty hysterical. During the bi-weekly process, it was tough stuff. I'd show up at eight. He'd have been there for a few hours already. We'd work until 1:00 or 2:00 in the afternoon. I'd make a FedEx run. I'd come back. He'd work through most of the night. I'd come back the next morning and there he'd be again. Incidentally, at one point we actually made it on the radio.[16]”

McFarlane wanted to leave his mark on the character. “I wanted to emphasize the ‘spider’ in the word Spider-Man. So I made his eyes a lot bigger to make them look like bug eyes. He has webbing on his costume - I made about five times as much. When somebody is getting slugged, they're flying across the room; they're not just falling over. If somebody gets hit by a ray gun or something, the guy is blasting.[17]”

Being an artist wasn’t enough though as McFarlane really wanted to write. All the greats before him were writer/artists, from Jack Kirby, John Byrne, Frank Miller, Will Eisner, Jim Starlin, Dave Sim, Howard Chaykin, George Perez, Walt Simonson and more. Even the late Alan Kupperberg, an artist often unfairly derided by many, was writing and drawing books for Marvel[18]. Marvel gave McFarlane a new book to write and draw, titled *Spider-Man*.

The *Spider-Man* title would be partially based upon a new Batman title, *Legends of The Dark Knight*, which had debuted in November 1989. The new Batman book featured stories that were designed to stand-alone from the regular Batman titles (*Batman* and *Detective Comics*), thus allowing the creative teams freedom to tell stories with the only restriction being Batman had to live at the end. Unlike *Legends of the Dark Knight,* which would have rotating creative teams doing short story arcs. *Spider-Man* was to be McFarlane’s alone.

At the time, McFarlane was circumspect when it came to the reasons why he was writing a new title. "I worked for Roy Thomas a few years and I had some contact with him because he was my editor, but I worked for like a year and a half with Peter David, then two years with Dave Michelinie, and you can almost count on one hand the amount of times I have talked to the writer. I kind of take a stance that I don't talk to the writers, tell them anything about their writing, and they don't have the right to talk to me about my artwork.

"I've found that the writers that I've worked for, especially David, actually wanted feedback from me. He wanted me to give him story ideas, he wanted me to have more input into it - but I kind of took that stance. And by the time that I felt that I had some ideas for the book, I felt it wouldn't be fair to him to, like, change the rules of the game. The book was doing okay with him doing the story and me doing the artwork, we weren't really suffering or anything like that. Maybe I frustrate the writers that I work for because I don't ever talk to them, but it's worked out for me. Everybody does their own thing.

"When I was penciling, the reason I broke in being a penciler was that I thought that most people would send in their samples because they think that they can do it better than the guys that are doing it, or most of the guys that are doing it. And the same thing happened with the inking, you know. I wasn't satisfied with the inking and I thought I could do something a little bit different and be a little more true to what I wanted on the page.

"And then once I became a little bit more adept at inking, it's like, 'Well, let's go to the next thing.' And right now the next thing is writing. After doing two years on the book, a lot of ideas that I have are stored in the back of my mind and there's only one way to get them on paper, that's to write them myself. It wouldn't be fair to David to all of a sudden graft my ideas to his. Maybe not, maybe that would have been the way to go, but I'm at the ballsy stage.[19]"

As time went on, and with the benefit of hindsight, McFarlane reflected on that period and gave more insight. "Just because I was always sort of a curious little kid, you know, I kept getting somebody else's stories and I wanted to write my own stories," said McFarlane in 2002. "And so knowing that something had to give, I walked away from *Amazing Spider-Man* and said, you know, I want to try and find a job that I can write and I don't want to - I don't want to write somebody else's stuff. And so I'll just quit and I'll go see if somebody will give me a job as a novice writer, if you will, but a skilled artist at this point and move from there.

"Given at that time *Spider-Man, Amazing Spider-Man*, was doing pretty good and I helped boost the sales on the book, they didn't want me to really leave *Spider-Man*. So I don't know what the origin of it was, but they had *Spider-Man* books and somebody figured out there's four weeks, so they went, 'Well, what if we let you stay on *Spider-Man*? We'll let you write it and we'll create a new *Spider-Man* book for you.'

"I mean, it was better, better than I'd ever thought. I thought I was falling into that part because it would be a big title and I was sort of a novice writer, but, of course, I enthusiastically said yes. And so I then became the writer, penciler, inker of a new title that was just called *Spider-Man*, so there were no adjectives in front of it.[20]"

The first issue of *Spider-Man* sold 3,000,000 copies. This was assisted by Marvel releasing it in multiple formats, a trend that would be repeated for later comics, amongst them Jim Lee's *X-Men* #1 and Rob Liefeld's *X-Force* #1. People didn't merely buy one copy of the book; they bought several, the bagged edition, the gold edition, the silver edition, the news-stand edition, the bagged news-stand edition and so on. Then people had to find the retailer only platinum edition, or the signed edition...it seemed endless.

Anything that McFarlane touched was an instant best seller. The newly formed *Wizard* magazine picked up on McFarlane as a fan favorite and sold him without a hint of shame[21]. The publisher of the magazine, Gareb Shamus, quickly became friends with McFarlane and even publicized this fact in the magazine, all the time promoting him by giving him the top spot in many of their polls.

Not everyone bought *Spider-Man* #1 to read. Many people bought it as an investment, buying multiples of each edition, bagging, boarding, and storing them in the hopes that, one day, the price would rise and the payoff would be immense. The speculator era had begun.

"I'm probably as surprised as anyone," he told the reporters who asked him for his reaction to the news. "Even though I love doing it and put a lot into my work it's still just a comic book. I mean, it's not like it's an oil painting or something.[22]"

"Now I can draw whatever I want," McFarlane told the *Ottowa Citizen*. "I try to put in everything I liked when I collected comics. My whole goal is to make it different than the other Spider-Man books.[23]"

"His powers – Extraordinary! His web-line – Advantageous!"[24] – *Spider-Man* #1

Those who did buy *Spider-Man* #1 to read were in for a rude shock. As great an artist that Todd McFarlane was considered to be, he was far from being a great, let alone competent, writer. The art looked great but the dialogue was laughable.

The one thing McFarlane was in dire need of was a strong editor. However he'd made it clear that wasn't going to happen.

"I could hire my mom to do what most of the editors in this business do," he said. "Editors are glorified babysitters to me - they don't add nothing, they don't do nothing, they get the books out on time and they're traffic managers. Every now and then, just so they can justify their paycheck to the big guys upstairs, they change something. Do they change it for the better? No, they change it for the sake of change. There's no reason behind most of their changes, other than when they get called on the carpet, and somebody says to them, "Why is the sales of Spider-Man going up twice as fast?" They can't say, "Well, I've got this creative guy that I don't do nothing with and I just let him do whatever he wants and the sales go up." That doesn't bode well for you when you're starting to meet the people who are signing your checks. So editors are afraid for their jobs and so what they do is they touch stuff so they can say they touched it and that's it. We don't even have enough space for me and my attitudes about editing.[25]"

His views aside, many in the industry felt that McFarlane's abilities as a writer were sorely lacking, and his place on the *Spider-Man* book was only due to his art.

Neil Gaiman would later recall the general attitude towards McFarlane's *Spider-Man*. "As a writer of comics, I would get the DC Comics, they send you everything they publish that month, and I saw *Infinity, Inc.* which was drawn by Todd, and later I remember somebody coming up to me in the DC offices showing me *Spider-Man* number 1, which Todd drew and which people thought was very funny because the writing demonstrated that the person writing it had never written anything before.[26]"

Not that McFarlane wasn't aware of his shortcomings, once boasting to Australian writer Dave deVries that he could draw a book of *Thor* picking his nose or a book of 22 pages, completely blank barring his autograph, and they'd sell. After selling 3,000,000 copies of a single book, very few people were game enough to tell McFarlane he couldn't write. But he knew. Dave deVries offered to proof read the book and suggest changes, uncredited, only to be told by McFarlane, "Why bother? It's gonna sell millions anyway[27]."

"I mean, fuck, I didn't let some little thing like not being able to write stop me, so I didn't really see where that should actually be that much of a problem," McFarlane told Gary Groth. "I just wanted to test to see how much balls people had. Some people had a fear, like 'Yeah, you're right, I can't write.' Well, OK, that's fine, then plot the thing and give it to a writer. And that's one of the reasons why I don't use a writer on my stuff: I think that's almost an insult to a writer for me to want to plot it and then just give it to them to put words to it. Even though they do a hell of a lot better job than I would.[28]"

McFarlane found that even his popularity had limits within company walls and that he'd not be able to draw whatever he wanted. He submitted the art for *Spider-Man* #16 only to have it sent back with instructions to re-draw it as it was too graphic for print. The offending piece of art showed the character Juggernaut being speared through the eye, with the spear emerging from the back of his head.

Exit wounds had been shown in Marvel previously, notably during Frank Miller's first *Daredevil* run. Miller often showed characters, notably Elektra, spearing others with martial arts weapons such as sais and swords, but each time he showed an exit wound, the wound was covered by clothing being stretched, often leading to general ridicule and questions being asked as to how a sai could be sharp enough to slide through flesh but be stopped by a rayon shirt. Now McFarlane knew the answer, because Marvel refused to show a proper exit wound.

"The Comics Code said you couldn't have an exit wound," McFarlane told the *Arizona Republic*. "But I could have drawn it in silhouette and it would have been ok. Either its ok or it isn't. I threw a temper tantrum and quit. Even that itself was symbolic because it was really a culmination of eight years of being rubbed the wrong way.[29]"

McFarlane had been looking for an excuse to take a break and plot his next move, and now he found it. Where Miller and others had simply dealt with and worked around the issue of the outdated Comics Code, McFarlane did the unimaginable: he not only quit *Spider-Man*, and Marvel Comics, he quit the comic book industry completely.

Forming Image

After quitting Marvel, McFarlane took time off to be with his family. With the money that he had earned, along with the cash that continued to pour in from Marvel, he could easily afford to reflect upon his next move, and he wanted his next move to be one of total control. One person he was talking to, who had the same kind of success, but was pilloried even more than Todd McFarlane and yet had a hide thicker than the average rhinoceros, was Rob Liefeld.

Liefeld and McFarlane had forged a friendship during their time at Marvel Comics. McFarlane would lend his inking talents to Liefeld's pencils for a handful of covers, including the now sought-after *New Mutants* #87, which featured the first appearance of *Cable*. Liefeld's covers were often hit or miss, but the addition of McFarlane's inks made them stand out. Liefeld was able to return the favor, inking two pages of *Spider-Man* #10 when McFarlane found himself up against a deadline[1].

At the time Liefeld, then hot off the *New Mutants* title, had taken over the mantle of the 'hottest' artist at Marvel, to the extent that Marvel, like they had done for McFarlane, had a created a new title just for him, called *X-Force*. This wasn't enough though. Liefeld wanted more creative control and less corporate input into what he was producing, and so the seeds for Image Comics were beginning to be sown.

"When I got on *The New Mutants* at Marvel, they really allowed me to let my imagination run loose," Liefeld said. "The sales had turned around on the comic book, so they let me do more and more. It quickly got to the point where I wanted to do much more. I wanted to produce comic books the way a movie producer produces movies, doing multiple projects at a time. I wanted to have a whole line of comics with all sorts of different characters, but that option wasn't available at Marvel at that time. They worried enough about you getting out your one comic book a month, and they got pretty uneasy about the prospect of me doing two, three, or four comics a month.[2]"

Before forming Image, McFarlane, Liefeld, Silvestri, Valentino, Larsen and Lee met with Marvel to formally quit the company. Marvel instantly organized a meeting with McFarlane, Liefeld and Lee to see if anything could be done to keep them in house. One idea that Marvel floated was that the artists take over the all but defunct Epic Comics line, owned by Marvel, and in which they would all share in character ownership. In effect, Epic would be Image, just distributed by Marvel. This idea was rejected outright.

"When Marvel offered us Epic, we knew we weren't even on the same page as Marvel," Liefeld said. "We didn't want to relaunch Epic for them, we wanted to have something new, to create a new prototype. And that's what we did and we had a lot of fun.[3]"

"Ever since there was anybody working on comics that fans gave a rat's ass about, the fans were always asking things like, 'Gee , I wonder what it would be like if John Buscema, Neal Adams, John Romita, and those other guys left to form their own company?'" Larsen later said. "The question sort of followed creators around as they came into prominence, and we were the first guys who said, 'Yeah, let's see what happens if we do form our own company.[4]'"

In 2002 McFarlane told the court about the formation of Image Comics. "I'd been having off and on conversations with sort of other free-lancers and friends about sort of saying, 'Why don't we start our own company. What are we working for the companies for? Sort of dancing to their tunes to some extent. Why don't go we go and try to band together.' And so by the end of 1991 we had gathered seven of us and three of us announced to Marvel that we were in unison leaving Marvel comic books to sort of start a commune of artists and writers together and that started, that began what we ended up calling it Image Comics and that began in 1992, the beginning of '92.

"Image was put together to sort of create a logo. You know, we had sort of a brand name. We as artists were not necessarily skilled in the details of business at this time and so we ended up running into some people that had a smaller company called Malibu Comics and they offered to publish the books for us to help us on our way; let us sort of as much as possible concentrate on doing the art, if you will, and the books and the writing and not worry about sort of the other things that are inherent with publishing a comic book. So each one of us went to our little hovels, started our own companies, created our own characters and then fed those ideas in the forms of comic books into this commune and then those were published by Malibu Comics starting in 1992.[5]"

The original Image was a collective formed by McFarlane, Jim Lee, Rob Liefeld, Marc Silvestri, Erik Larsen and Jim Valentino. "Everybody had their own thing," Valentino said. "Some people wanted to build empires, some wanted to create multimedia properties, and some wanted a place where they could just work on their own comic book for the rest of their lives. But, overall, Image is a place where people can control their own creative destinies, and that's what started it all off.[6]"

Long time X-Men writer Chris Claremont and artist Whilce Portacio were also announced as being part of the start-up of Image, but it wasn't to be. Portacio quickly dropped out due to personal reasons and Claremont never formally signed on, although he would reunite with Jim Lee to work on the latter's flagship book, *W.I.L.D.Cats*.

Not everyone was entirely sure that this was the right idea. While Lee, Liefeld and McFarlane had financial security, the others weren't as assured. Silvestri and Larsen weren't struggling, but Valentino had been down this road previously, having entered the comic book industry with his creator owned *normalman*, which was published first by Dave Sim and then Sim's wife, Deni Loubert.

Adding to the worry was that not everyone left Marvel on their own terms. In Valentino's case, he was pushed out.

"It was dreadfully frightening for me," Valentino said. "In the first place, I was fired from my Marvel title. I didn't want to leave it. Also, my Marvel title wasn't a mega-seller, so I didn't have a huge bankroll or fan base to rely on. For me, it was really, really difficult. We almost lost our house that first year. It was a very big gamble.[7]"

For all his success, Lee also had very real concerns. "Certainly, there was trepidation," Lee recalled. "Failing was one of my biggest fears. I felt that, if we failed, we'd still have careers in comics but we'd be blacklisted, and they would make it hard for us to come back right away.[8]"

Liefeld, Silvestri and MacFarlane had no such fears. "I just wanted to be able to go and do something new, and I really didn't care about the payday or the sales," Liefeld said. "I knew I could be making less money, but the benefits that I had at the time were that I was single and I was just 22 years old. I remember thinking that, if I fell flat on my face, I'd just get up again. I can understand the feelings and considerations of the other guys with wives and kids, though. I remember thinking that it was a much tougher choice for them than for me. I couldn't even possibly have put myself in that position.[9]"

"At that time (and this isn't even with the benefit of 20/20 hindsight)", Silvestri would say, "it seemed like a no-lose situation for us. The market was perfect, the people involved were perfect, and the timing was perfect.[10]"

McFarlane had the most to lose, and yet had the most confidence out of the original seven. After giving Jim Lee a pep talk ("I told him, you're Jim Frigging Lee,"), McFarlane settled in. "I would probably say that, out of all of us, I knew this was going to work," he remembered. "In my mind there was no risk. Was there a risk that we'd sell less than we were selling at Marvel and end up making less money? Well, yeah, but to me that wasn't even a factor. When you really get tired of your job, you'd take a pay cut in a heartbeat just to get away from it. When I quit Marvel, I was the top-paid guy in the country and I couldn't spend all the money they were paying me, so in terms of the economic risk, I'd been saving my Spidey money.[11]"

The six Image creators all had their own studios. McFarlane owned Todd McFarlane Productions, Jim Lee had WildStorm Productions, Larsen owned Highbrow Entertainment, Valentino owned Shadowline, Silvestri owned Top Cow Productions, and Liefeld owned Extreme Studios.

It was announced that all six Image founders would all launch a new title with Image, with original, never before seen, characters. This wasn't exactly true as Liefeld's *Youngblood* had appeared as early as 1987 in the pages of *Megaton Comics Explosion* #1 published by Megaton Comics, and Larsen's *Savage Dragon* dated back to 1982 when Larsen debuted the character in his own self-published title, *Graphic Fantasy*. McFarlane's title was *Spawn*. Although appearing for the first time, *Spawn* had been created, at least visually, by McFarlane as far back as his (McFarlane) high school days and bore striking similarities to a *Spider-Man* villain, *The Prowler* whose costume and look had been redesigned by McFarlane, complete with flowing cape and stylized costume.

Coming with McFarlane from his early days were Al Simmons and Terry Fitzgerald. "Out of the blue, I got home from college one day. It must have been November or December 1991," recalled Fiztgerald. "There's a message on the answering machine. 'I got a question. I got some work for you. Give me a call.' So I phone. He wanted to do these hockey trading cards for the NHL. He didn't have enough time to do preliminary sketches and design work. I did ten or twenty of these. Nothing really happened after that until I got a phone call around late March/early April 1992. Todd said he quit *Spider-Man*. He was doing this new book called *Spawn*. He gave me a little background on that. He was moving to Portland. I said, if I'm ever down in California, I'll drop by. He said, 'No, I was actually thinking you could come and work for me.' That was the sales ticket. I wanted to come in five minutes.[12]"

The new titles from Image were launched with some controversy.

"I think that in many ways we've been holding back," said Erik Larsen. "Most of our best creations have yet to be seen and will be seen under the Image imprint for the first time. We're really going to turn some heads with this stuff. We haven't wanted to give away our creations to the big companies. This setup is ideal. We can share one universe just as we would at the 'big two' plus we can retain full ownership of whatever characters we create - It's fantastic! And it helps that Rob, Todd and I are buddies to begin with. This is the most exciting thing to happen to comics since the creation of the Marvel Universe.[13]"

Larsen's claim that the Image founders had been 'holding back' while working at Marvel and DC drew criticism from some high-profile creators who were entrenched at the two companies. Writer Peter David took particular exception to the comments and fired back in the pages of the *The Incredible Hulk*. Challenged to a formal debate with McFarlane at the 1993 Comicfest, David figuratively tore McFarlane apart. This only seemed to anger Larsen more, and the feud between Larsen and David continued in the pages of their respective titles, letter pages and David's own regular column in *The Comic Buyer's Guide*.

Creating *Spawn*

***Spawn* is** Todd McFarlane's baby. It is the one thing that nobody can take away from him, claim credit for, or ownership of.

McFarlane later gave his reason as to why *Spawn* never saw print before Image. "'Why didn't a guy like Todd McFarlane, one of your more commercial talents out there, why did he never pull *Spawn* out of his portfolio? And as a matter of fact, why didn't he ever create a new character for these companies, period?' I mean, after a year and a half on *Spider-Man*, I could have created twenty new characters. But you never saw one new character from me. No - I made up my mind a long time ago not to. Being the psychotic shit that I was - and having read all the interviews - I knew that Jack Kirby got fucked. That was the biggest revelation for me: if The King can get fucked, anybody can get fucked! I always knew going in - from day one - that I wanted to start a union. Except nobody gave a shit, because back when I started on *Infinity, Inc*. I was a nobody. So I'm just saying today the same things I said five years ago. The voice is the same.[1]"

McFarlane took on the role of writer and artist of *Spawn*, keeping in line with other Image founders. For him, the concept of *Spawn* was as simple as could be. It was a love story, from Todd to Wanda.

"For me, at its core, its simplest overview, it's a love story," McFarlane told the court in 2010. "The main concept of *Spawn* is that he literally trades everything at a moment of death to come back to see his wife one last time. I think most of us put in that position would probably do the same thing. I have a wife that I love dearly. The wife in this comic book is called Wanda, the name of my wife, so I sort of draw from things in my personal life.

"And then you take that piece of the story, which is, I betrayed everything to come back to my own life -- and you go, fine, sign on the dotted line, which is the deal we make with the devil. And you come back and the world is topsy-turvy and now what do you do? You find out that your wife, the only thing you came back for, this love, this great love of yours, she is now remarried, she has had a child. He wasn't able to bear children with her.

"And now he finds out he has got these fantastic powers -- and I will get into the comic book part of it -- he has these fantastic powers. His identity has been stripped from him. He has no skin. He is not recognizable.

"And now he goes, 'Wow! The one thing I wanted to do was just to get back to my wife. She has got children, which makes her happy. She is married to a good guy, which is my best friend. So of all the guys in the world that I would like to take care of my wife that would be him. And now I have got all of these sort of crazy powers and forces, no identity, what now?' And it just becomes the beginning of the journey of the hero quest.

"I set out when I left Marvel to create a character that is African American but get rid of the one thing that we have a tendency to do when we look at people that aren't the same as us, is we just make instant judgment. And the reason we don't like people of color is because of the color of their skin, so just made a solution, strip the skin off it, get away from that.

"Every time in comic book history they try to do something that is a minority character, they draw attention to it. I wanted to actually be the opposite. I wanted to sort of take that piece and make it go away so that Spawn just became this hero, regardless of whatever his skin color was. So besides my personal philosophical input, the other part is just, 'You want to go see your wife? Ha-ha-ha! I'm the devil. I'm going to trick you. I'm going to strip your skin off you. And even if you go see her, she is never going to recognize you.'[2]"

The Image creators met with mixed reactions to their respective books. The art was of the era: flashy, loud and big. It either left people cold or invigorated them. Most people felt that the company was a gimmick and would not last without the kind of support that Marvel or DC could provide.

"When Image started," Neil Gaiman recalled, "they were getting a lot of stick from fans and from the comics press for being illiterate garbage, which is probably a polite way of putting the things they were saying about the comics, chiefly those written by Rob Liefeld.[3]"

Not that accusations of poor writing bothered anybody at Image. Indeed, they put such claims down to one thing: jealousy. "I don't care what anybody said it was," McFarlane said, "it was pure jealousy. I know they didn't think we could draw, I know they didn't think we could write, I know they didn't think we could tie our own shoes, but they'd have taken our comic book that sold a million in a heartbeat.[4]"

Silvestri agreed. "It was jealousy, pure and simple. There were some very outspoken critics, and the bright green color of their skin became very apparent to everybody. Sorry if they take it the wrong way, but we made fun of them on a daily basis, and a lot of people who weren't even involved with Image made fun of them. We had a few good laughs about them but didn't take them seriously.[5]"

The one thing that critics of *Spawn* could not deny was the sheer popularity of the title. The first issue sold an amazing 1,700,000 copies, a record for an independent title. Priced at $1.95, McFarlane earned the lion's share of the profits, proving, once again, that everything he touched turned to gold.

Sadly, the early days of Image weren't all wine and roses. Books came out late, in some cases titles were solicited and pre-orders taken only for the books never to appear. McFarlane, Larsen and Lee did their best to carry the line with regular books, but even McFarlane found himself behind schedule and tapped Grant Morrison and Greg Capullo to quickly work up three fill-in issues while he took time out to draw the Frank Miller scripted *Spawn/Batman*.

No matter the merits of the books produced, Image promised that any creator who worked under their umbrella would completely own their characters and work, unlike other companies. They would also be paid and treated better than they ever had been by the likes of Marvel and DC. These points, and the fact that McFarlane appeared to fail in adhering to them, would prove important with his later battles with Neil Gaiman.

Despite the naysayers, *Spawn* has lasted the distance, as has another Image comic, Erik Larsen's *Savage Dragon*. However, unlike *Savage Dragon*, *Spawn* has made the jump from comic book to feature film. To be fair, there was an animated *Dragon* series, but then there was an animated *Spawn* series as well. In short, if Image has a flagship character, and title, it's *Spawn*. By 1996, *Spawn* was selling an average of 160,000 books per month.

Naming *Tony Twist*

> "Twist is the Mafia Don of the greater New York area, and takes any assault on his power very personally. After the *Violator* killed several of his men, Twist mistakenly attributed the killing to *Spawn*, who had just made his first appearance. A war was declared on *Spawn* and Twist hired the Cybernetic mercenary *Overt-kill* to hunt and slaughter *Spawn*. *Spawn* has made several direct threats to Twist, and Twist has reluctantly called off his vendetta against *Spawn*. However, he is constantly scheming and planning new ways to destroy *Spawn*.[1]"

As well as creating *Spawn* and his backstory, McFarlane also created a rogues gallery. Characters such as *Clown, Violator, Overt-Kill* and even Satan himself would appear to battle *Spawn*. As well as fighting super villains and creatures from Hell, *Spawn* also battled more earthly villains. And it was here that McFarlane made the first of three errors that would cost him dearly for years to come.

When it came to naming characters, McFarlane stuck to a tried and true formula for him – he named his characters after real people. Over the years people saw their names appear in his comic books, along with their images (that practice went back to his days on the *Hulk*) and most were flattered or, at the very least, amused at seeing themselves immortalized in a comic book.

Usually these were people he knew; *Spawn*'s name was Al Simmons, a childhood friend of McFarlane's. Simmons was thrilled when he learnt the news. "When he called me up he did not tell me I was going to be the lead character," he said. "But I was honored by it. I mean, my name was going to be in a comic by Todd McFarlane. I thought it was just going to be something like 'And then the garbage truck ran over Al Simmons...' It's a real honor. I mean, sports figures become like superheroes, but to be named a 'real' superhero is a real honor.[2]"

Spawn's wife, Wanda, was named for Todd's wife Wanda Kolomyjec, whom he'd known since childhood. The pair had met when Wanda was thirteen and have been together ever since. "I'm not sure the character is any more closely related (to me) than just the name," Kolomyjec said. "Same thing with the little girl (in the comic) named Cyan, although with Cyan it was a little more immortalized because when he started *Spawn*, he made Cyan the character the age that our daughter was at the same time. A lot of the stuff that you read in that book where she's doing things and saying things Todd did pick up from our daughter.[3]"

Other people had mixed feelings on the subject. Some were less than amused, some chose to ignore it and others wanted to take serious action.

"Several years back I got an angry phone call from John Byrne, and for a refreshing change of pace, he wasn't angry at me," McFarlane's former *Hulk* writer Peter David would later write. "'Did you read *Spawn* #30?' he asked. In *Spawn* #30, there were two members of the Ku Klux Klan, and their names were Peter and Johnny. Byrne was convinced that Todd McFarlane, *Spawn* creator, writer and erstwhile penciler, had dubbed the characters thusly for the purpose of taking a direct swipe at us. After all, Byrne and I had not marched in the preferred lockstep of approval for all things Image that the founders seemed to desire of the comic pro community. Byrne felt that it was nothing less than character assassination, was contemplating taking direct legal action, and wanted to know if I would be interested in joining him in such an endeavor.

"I demurred, citing the following reasons. First, since it was only our first names, it couldn't be proven absolutely that it was intended to be us. Second, although associating us with the KKK was distasteful, there was nothing illegal about belonging to that notorious organization, and if you wanted to be rock solid for getting damages in a libel action, the person you were accusing had to have accused you of criminal activity. Third, there was no way we were going to prove damages, because there was no way we were going to get a witness on a stand who was going to state that Todd's juvenile jab had cost Byrne or I employment. And fourth... it's Todd McFarlane, fer cryin' out loud. Who cares what he thinks?[4]"

In the sixth issue of *Spawn*, McFarlane introduced a mobster to serve as a villain for Spawn. This would be the first of McFarlane's biggest mistakes. McFarlane named the mobster Antonio Twistelli, aka Tony Twistelli, or, as he became known, Tony Twist. There was one problem, the real Tony Twist existed and was known to McFarlane. He was a hockey player, an enforcer, more commonly known as a 'goon'.

As McFarlane envisioned him, Antonio Twistelli was a large man, akin to the *Spider-Man* and *Daredevil* foe *The Kingpin*, only with hair, glasses and a dark suit, and with a toothpick between his teeth, which often hovered in mid-air, suspended if you will, while Twist screamed at someone handy. The character was a cliché at best and not one of McFarlane's best efforts as a creator.

Tony Twist, in the comic, was an evil mob leader, prone to such doltims as, "Make sure he suffers before you kill him. Then bring me his heart." "Now let us vote. Do we continue letting some back-alley hero keep killing us, or do we dispose of the parasite?[5]" and "If I find out he's in any way connected to our mysterious hero, his balls are mine! Hell! Even if he's not connected, we'll dust him anyways! A few deaths should do the job.[6]"

Unfortunately for McFarlane, he didn't reach out to talk to the real Tony Twist before publication. "I do lots of products, I have a lot of employees, and that one time on one page, one person making an opinion doesn't speak for the whole, but overall, I've never spoken to Mr. Twist prior to this lawsuit.[7]"

McFarlane could have saved himself millions of dollars simply by picking up the phone, but he didn't.

Writing *Spawn*

> "And so it goes. Antonio Twist tries to swallow up more power. His nickname on the street is 'Dracula' because he lives to suck the power out of everyone. He considers his options, which companies to engulf; what to wear to the charity fundraiser; whose wife to seduce.[1]"

One thing that almost everybody, including some of those directly involved, could agree on was that the overall writing on those early books left a lot to be desired. The quality of writing in Image Comics in the early days wasn't overly respected, both amongst peers and the public, but that didn't stop the fans, an especially the speculators from buying anything with the Image logo on it by the hundreds of thousands.

"*Spawn* had been out for maybe about a year at this point or close to it and Image Comics was founded by a bunch of artists and the knock against us was that, you know, we didn't know how to write," McFarlane told the courts. "We could only draw. And so again it would be -- I thought it would be sort of an interesting idea to bring some writers on to on to the book to sort of see what their take would be on some of the ideas for it. I came with a mental list of guys that sort of would fit the bill, that would sort of be interesting names to put on it and then started making phone calls.[2]"

It was the accusations of producing garbage that saw McFarlane approach Neil Gaiman, Frank Miller, Dave Sim and Alan Moore with offers for each to write one-off issues of Spawn.

“I'm the kind of guy that phones a lot of people, and if I phone Alan Moore and ask him to write me a story and he says "no," then I didn't have him before the phone call so I'm no worse for wear,” McFarlane said at the time. “And I can be pretty convincing when I get on the phone or whatever. So I just phone people up and it's like, "Hey, you don't know me, I don't know you, but we know each other's work, blah, blah, blah, blah, blah, have I got a proposition for you. I know you like to do this. I think I've got a character that kind of fits into what you do, blah, blah, blah," and I just be a good salesman and they all... I mean I had a list of four and I hit four for four. My attitude when I'm talking to people is that the last topic of conversation is finances, 'cause I don't want a guy to do work for money, I want a guy to do work 'cause he likes it. So when I talk to them I'd like, I know that Alan Moore likes to write some horror stuff and stuff that's a bit off center, so I come at I'm like ‘This is my character, this is what he can do, here's the things that I think would work and I know that you like to write these kinds of stories, but I think that my guy has enough layers involved that I think that there's something there for you to play with, and we'd have a hell of a ride.’[3]”

Out of the four, the only person McFarlane had worked with, albeit peripherally, was Frank Miller when McFarlane assisted Klaus Janson by filling in blacks during the inking stage on Miller's *‘The Dark Knight Returns’*. McFarlane's name had also been linked with Miller's when, in 1989, it was announced at the San Diego Comic Con that Miller would be writing a proposed *Batman/Spider-Man* cross-over, to be drawn by McFarlane and scripted by Steve Gerber. Sadly, that book never got past the rumor stage, but it had the potential to have been a magnificent thing to see.

The four men took on the job for various reasons.

“It should be very educational for both of us (me and Todd that is),” Gaiman said in 1992. “I think it's going to be fun. It's about angels. There's going to be lots of hitting and shouting and running around, which will be a first for me. Todd said I could write an entire issue of Spawn where somebody sat and read a newspaper. He'd do it. It was my deal.[4]”

“I mean, it seems Alan Moore and Neil Gaiman are pretty much the same type of writer,[5]" was McFarlane's blunt assessment at the time.

Money was definitely a reason as McFarlane promised a huge payday for a single issue.

"I told them that they would get $100,000 for doing it and in a sense it was pretty much the same conversation for everybody," McFarlane recalled. "I wanted them to be equal, so did all of them, so they could pass notes back and forth. And so we started from there.[6]"

"There was no initial discussion of payment amounts," Gaiman remembered. "As I recall, when I agreed to do it, I got a check and a call from Terry Fitzgerald, who worked for Todd in some capacity, which rather surprised me, but this was after I had agreed to do it, sending a check for $10,000 for having agreed to do it and saying that when the script came in, there will be another $10,000 and then after that there would be a royalty that would come in on the issue. And when it became apparent that the orders of the issue were, according to them, I believe 1.1 million copies, they said it was going to be around $100,000, which would be the kind of royalty that you would have got from any publisher on those kind of sales, but none of the financial details were discussed with Todd in those early phone calls.[7]"

The offer of $100,000 would be the same for all four writers, a sign of parity and solidarity for the four writers, who knew that, as good as Dave Sim was as a writer, his contribution wouldn't sell as many as the more popular Miller, Moore and Gaiman.

The four issues were as different from each other as could be, and, as an experiment, or stunt (take your pick), they were successful with each issue selling over a million copies each. Moore elected to write a story taking place in Hell, involving a child killer that had been killed previously by *Spawn*. Miller's story saw him in familiar territory, writing about an urban gang war that had broken out in the alley where *Spawn* resided.

Dave Sim's story was the most unusual. "It's 22 pages of a political soapbox for Dave," McFarlane said. "It works! It's too funny; this is too cool. It's got Wonder Woman in it, it's got Batman, it's got the Thing - it's got everybody in it. It's a keeper for the ages. What made me include Dave? Two reasons: #1, he's Canadian; and #2, he's always been a fuck and I kind of admire guys like him.[8]"

Sim took the opportunity provided by the platform of large Image readership to promote creators' rights, with Sim's character, *Cerebus*, teaching *Spawn* a valuable lesson in the topic. Even more fascinating is that Sim had McFarlane draw arms of characters from Marvel and DC in full costume, including *Superman,* who delivers a lecture, albeit with logos and faces in heavy shadow. Even though the characters were easily identifiable by their limbs, neither Marvel nor DC took any form of action.

Out of the four special issues, Neil Gaiman's storyline would have the longest lasting effect upon the *Spawn* universe.

Creating *Angela*

Neil Gaiman's story, *Angela*, saw the introduction of new characters, notably *Medieval Spawn* and two new *Spawn* foes, in the form of angels, *Angela* and *Gabrielle*. Moore and Miller had elected not to create any new characters and Sim used his own.

After the issues were finished and published, the four writers went their own ways. Alan Moore remained with Image, electing to return to the superhero genre with a touching homage to the Marvel comics of the 1960s, as written and drawn by Stan Lee, Jack Kirby, Dick Ayers and Steve Ditko, by co- creating and writing a new series for Image, titled *1963*.

1963 would see Moore working with previous artistic collaborators in the form of Dave Gibbons (*Watchmen*), Stephen Bissette (*Swamp Thing*), Rick Vietch and John Totleben (both from *Miracleman* and *Swamp Thing*), as well as contributions from Don Simpson, Murphy Anderson, Melinda Gebbie and Jim Valentino. It was intended to be a mini-series, with an annual to bring the characters into the 'modern' Image Universe. It wasn't to be as the Image founders all appeared to wage an ongoing war for Moore's services[1] and the final annual, to be published by Jim Lee's Wildstorm[2], was never completed.

Frank Miller dabbled with Image, notably on a *Batman/Spawn* crossover, again with McFarlane on art chores. Although he provided the occasional pin-up, Miller largely kept his distance, preferring to concentrate on his creator-owned series *Sin City* for Dark Horse.

Dave Sim, after donating his entire fee to the Comic Book Legal Defense Fund, went back his regular *Cerebus* series.

Neil Gaiman was given an offer from McFarlane to continue with his *Angela* creation in the form of a three-issue mini-series which he accepted.

"I've given him (McFarlane) far more plot than he can use in one issue in terms of various philosophical backgrounds to Spawn's universe," said Gaiman. "There's an awful lot more there than I will be able to get in to my story, which has a working title of *And Men Shall Call Her Angela* (because I've always wanted to write a story called *And Men Shall Call Her Angela*![3]"

Character ownership wasn't discussed. "Essentially, the way that I'm working is something like this," McFarlane said at the time. "I divide the money up between the guy who writes, pencils, inks it, and the guy who created it, you know what I mean. And the guy who created it gets basically the least amount of it. So, if somebody decides to do an issue of *Spawn* then I get a little piece just because of advertising, and I laid the groundwork, and I did the first twelve issues. But other than that, you know, this isn't about money, it's about keeping the legend going.[4]"

Why did Neil Gaiman create characters for *Spawn* where Moore, Miller and Sim didn't?

For one, it wasn't just the money.

"If memory serves, I had received more than that ($100,000) for *Black Orchid*, which was a three-issue series that I had done for DC in 1988. As a novelist, I received significantly more than that. As for a one-shot story, it was significantly more than I had received for one comic. Having said that, I had not written at the time, nor had I had any interest in writing comics that would have sold in the numbers that *Spawn* was. And also, we were in the middle, actually that was – we weren't even in the middle, that was the high point of -- you can actually go back and look at the graph. That was the high point of what was called the speculator boom. So that payment would have been very comparable to anything coming out then as a number one or with a foil-embossed cover or anything. Comics were selling 750,000 to 1.5 million copies. These days 100,000 is incredibly good. These days 40,000 is really good.[5]"

Part of the reason was down to McFarlane's persistence. Once he realized what he wanted, he'd stop at nothing to get it. At his 2002 deposition, Gaiman gave an incredible insight into how McFarlane operated in 1993.

"Before I got the work, before I agreed to do it, there were several phone calls from Todd promising things and trying to persuade me to do it. From my perspective, there were a number of downsides to working with Todd and to working with Image. They were, despite their obvious commercial success, the industry laughing stock at the time, which meant that by working with them, by putting Mr. McFarlane in the position where he could use as his sole advertisement for *Spawn* 9, a black page with the word Gaiman written on it, that was something that was lending him cache and I had to decide whether or not I was willing to do that. So Todd was very much courting me. He very wisely didn't mention money at the time. What he talked to me about was showing unity with creators, sticking it to the big companies, complete creative freedom, not signing anything away, and just being, and also just pointing out that it would shake people up.

"And I think on the second phone call, when I was still wavering, he also said 'Okay, you know, I think I have got Alan Moore and I think Dave Sim and Frank Miller are going to say yes. Come on, it's the big four, you can't be left out.' And those were the things that he used to persuade me. I remember him offering complete creative freedom. The phrase he used was 'You can have 22 pages of *Spawn* reading the newspaper for all I care. You can make up his past, you can do whatever you like, you have complete creative freedom.' And I said yes in the end.

"Money was not discussed. The point money was discussed was after that first check came in with a little note from Terry Fitzgerald after I had done the first, my first sort of brainstorming. I had just brainstormed, said here is an idea, here is an idea, here is an idea and sent it off to them. And I got this check. And the next time Todd phoned, I said 'By the way, you know, you sent me a check, you haven't sent me any kind of contract.' And Todd said 'We don't send contracts, we treat you better, you know, it's just that's not how we do business, we don't do contracts, but we will treat you' -- he said 'But I will tell you what, I will treat you better than DC ever would with their contracts.' And that was the sum total of it. And I thought okay. And I sent my agent, Merrilee Heifetz, my literary agent, her share of the money, her 10 percent. And she phoned me up and said 'Where is the contract that goes with this?' And I said 'There is no contract. Todd has said he is going to treat me better than anybody would with a contract.' And she said 'You trust him?' And I said 'Yeah, he seems like a very good guy on the phone and he is not asking me to sign anything away.' So obviously I trusted him. And that was where we got up to at that point and that was the entire conversation about money.

"This is what Todd told me at the time, the orders for *Spawn* 6 or 7 were down to about 600,000 copies. And with the Alan Moore issue, they went up to about 1.2 million. And for me they were about 1.1 million. So they doubled as a result of the gimmick. And Dave Sim came in at about 800,000 and Frank Miller's was up there around a million. And he decided to just, said "I'm just giving you all $100,000." And this was after the orders had started coming in and he saw what was actually happening. And he said 'I'm just going to give you all $100,000 rather than do the sums, so you have each got a round number and you can do with it what you will.' And I did the sums in my head, figured 1.1 million, $1.95 comics, 100,000 seemed about comparable to the kind of money I would be getting from DC, if I decided to write a number one for them at that point and, yeah, left it about there. I had recently done, about that time, I did *Sandman* number 50, our 50th anniversary edition, which came out with a special cover, extra length issue, and that at the time had sold over a quarter of a million copies. So, you know, you were looking at a 30, $40,000 royalty check on that. So it was definitely comparable.[6]"

If it wasn't for the money, and certainly not for the fame, as Gaiman was one of the 'Big Four' that McFarlane spoke about, why did Gaiman's work differ in content so much from the other three?

In 1993 Miller, Moore and Sim had all been around the block several times, so to speak. All had created original characters with varying degrees of success and control. Out of the three, Sim had been the most successful in retaining ownership of his work. *Cerebus The Aardvark* began as a creator owned comic book in 1977 and, despite overtures from the major companies, Sim kept strict control over the book and his character. Such was his knowledge of the issues faced by comic book creators that he was one of the leading lights, along with Scott McCloud, Steve Bissette, Larry Marder, Rick Veitch, Peter Laird, and Kevin Eastman in the drafting of the *A Bill of Rights for Comics Creators* document. As someone who had strict control over his work, there was no way that Sim would have considered creating a new character. He was willing to allow McFarlane the one time use of *Cerebus* though.

Miller was, at the time, one of the biggest names in the comic book industry. He had made a huge impact upon the medium with his *Daredevil* run for Marvel Comics. It was within the confines of that title that he created *Elektra*, allegedly gaining assurances from Marvel that the character would only ever be written and/or drawn by himself. Moving to DC Comics, he created *Ronin*, a series that he retained ownership of. Shortly after *Ronin* came the landmark *Batman* mini-series, *The Dark Knight Returns*. This book, written and penciled by Miller, with inks by Klaus Janson and colors by Lynn Varley, shook the American comic book industry. Miller returned to Marvel for another landmark *Daredevil* run, this time as writer only, and, in 1990, he wrote and drew the *Elektra Lives Again* graphic novel.

The popularity of both Miller and *Elektra* saw Marvel resurrect the character, an act that Miller considered a gross betrayal of the original promise. Now firmly entrenched at Dark Horse with his *Sin City* series, along with writing various other books, and the occasional *RoboCop* film, Miller wasn't about to hand McFarlane any new characters that he'd have no control over.

When it came to character creation, in 1993, Alan Moore stood head and shoulders above the others. From his early days writing for *2000AD, Warrior,* Marvel UK and other UK publishers, Moore had left behind a plethora of creations and concepts, none of which he owned. Moving to DC Comics, Moore began work on *Swamp Thing* where, again, he began to litter the book with his own characters, notably *John Constantine*, and concepts that the company would continue to mine for years to come. It was at DC that Moore, working with Dave Gibbons, created the series that he would be best known for, *Watchmen*.

Much like the Marvel *Elektra* deal and Frank Miller, DC Comics promised Moore and Gibbons a reversion of rights to *Watchmen* if the series ever fell out of print. Moore and Gibbons agreed to this, only to under-estimate the popularity of the story. The first issue of *Watchmen* appeared in September 1986, and, to date, the series has been reprinted at least 24 times by DC Comics in trade paperback format. Various offers have been tabled since, but the rights remain firmly in DC Comics grasp. A similar deal was offered to Moore and artist David Lloyd for *V For Vendetta*.

Moore, having seen some of his best creations taken from in the form of *Watchmen, V For Vendetta, Halo Jones, Miracleman* and more, wasn't about to create any new characters without retaining some form of ownership.

Neil Gaiman wasn't as jaded as his peers and was genuinely interested the *Spawn* universe. For him, the offer wasn't just another pile of money for a script; it was an opportunity to leave a mark on a book that he would probably never work on again.

In 2002 Gaiman gave his reasons for wanting to write *Spawn*.

"I was the writer of a comic named *Sandman*, which in 1992 was the single-most acclaimed ongoing series of comics probably that there has ever been in terms of literary rewards received and respect in the industry and personal awards that were corning in for the comic and for the writing thereof. Sandman slowly worked its way up from the first issue through to the last issue, from, on a league table of one to 500 being all the comics published that month, we started probably in the low nineties and slowly over the next seven years worked our way up more or less to number one. Since that time *Sandman* has been collected in trade paperback and has gone on to continue to sell millions of trade paperbacks.

"Todd phoned me up and asked me if I would consider writing an issue of *Spawn*. And all, as far as I know the Image people, they were all artists. He said what he wanted to do was go to the four best, biggest and most important writers in comics and get a guest issue written by each of them to show people that an Image comic could be well written and to show his, I don't think he used the word humility, it's not a word that Todd would use, but that was what was being communicated, that hey, I can learn, that kind of thing.

"I also think he considered it the ultimate marketing gimmick to have good writing. He said at one point to me during this that Liefeld and co were putting foil-embossed stamped covers on things and rolling out new number ones in order to get the numbers. And he had four issues of good writers and that was his gimmick.

"I asked Todd to explain *Spawn* to me. And he said *Spawn* was a CIA operative, he is dead, he gets killed, and he goes to hell. And the devil, who at that point he didn't have a name for, actually Alan Moore called him the *Malebolgia*, has sent him back to earth with a limited power thing and he is training to be in the Army of Hell. It was very important he was part of the Army of Hell.

“And I said to Todd ‘Okay. And who are they fighting?’ And Todd said ‘I don't know.’ And I thought about it a little. And I thought well, this wasn't talking to Todd, this was on my own, I thought well, you don't have an Army to fight librarians. If you are putting together the Army of Hell, one assumes that they are there at some point to fight the Army of Heaven, and that if you have an Army, heaven's army is worse. I thought cool, that gives me an angle.

“And I thought well, is there any reason why the angel can't be female. They were, up to that point, I think Todd sent me three or four issues of *Spawn* at that point, whatever was published. There were no women anywhere in them except for *Spawn's* ex-wife that I remember. I thought well; let's create a fun female character who is a kick ass angel. And I thought Todd didn't have a lot in terms of *Spawn* background story at that point. He had his situation, CIA, guy dies, goes to hell, comes back, is no longer, you know, is super powered dead thing whose life has moved on, and he had a scenario.

“From talking to him, it became apparent he didn't have anywhere he was going with it and he didn't have much in the way of background. So I thought it would be a good thing to give him background and to do the kinds of stuff for him that I would do for me in an issue of *Sandman*, where I will set up, you know, you will toss out a dozen things knowing that in two years' time, or a year's time, or six years' time or whatever, you may need them.[7]”

In short, Gaiman hadn’t been ripped off, either knowingly or unknowingly, enough, to hold back at this stage in his career. Which is not to say that Gaiman was naive, far from it.

“(In regards to the) 2000 AD stuff that was published, I rapidly realized that they were taking all rights to the work I did. At that point I think it was Fleetway Publications. One had to sign over all rights and I saw stories I had written reprinted in American editions and that they gave me no copies of and that I was not paid for. I spoke to Steve MacManus, the editor, who said that was how they did it and they would love to change it, but it wasn't changed. And that was the last thing I did for 2000 AD. After doing those four, maybe five stories for 2000 A.D., I washed my hands of them, have not worked for Fleetway since, have not submitted work for Fleetway since, have not gone back and looked at, nor could I find, I suspect, these days, any pieces of paper signed with Fleetway since, and chalked them up to experience as a bad job.[8]"

Hiring Gaiman as a writer for one issue of *Spawn* would eventually come back to haunt McFarlane as the second worse decision he made on *Spawn*, as Gaiman later sued McFarlane for characters that he (Gaiman) created, resulting in the *Miracleman* trial which would see McFarlane lose more than just money.

McFarlane was happy with Gaiman's efforts. "Number 9 is a good story, a good *Spawn* story so to speak. There's a bit of a flash back that shows that there's been Spawns in the past. But then it comes back to the present day and our *Spawn*, the one that was in the first seven issues, gets in a fight and does the comic book thing and whatever. That's one that Neil Gaiman's writing. And then for Neil, that's something that he's not really used to writing and so it gives him a chance to try something new and different himself.[9]"

But did McFarlane deliberately set out to steal from, or rip off, Neil Gaiman?

Simply put, no. From the beginning, McFarlane believed in what he, and Image Comics, were doing. Image and McFarlane both were righteous and would protect and nurture those creators who came over to them. They would be better for them, in the long run, than Marvel or DC Comics ever could be.

"What's going to allow us to compete in the long run and I'll believe this to my dying day - is the talent base that we have," McFarlane told the authors of *Comic Book Rebels*. "Because we're pro-creator. Now, that doesn't mean we can't each try to create our own universal character like *Mickey Mouse*, but what's going to get Image in the same ballgame is not that we have huge corporate backing, or a firm of forty-five lawyers; we don't have any of that. But you know what I think we're going to have in the long run? The most talent. And you know the only way we're going to keep attracting that top talent? On a basic level, there're only two things that really motivate most creative people: a) the bills getting paid or b) creative freedom.

"And we can offer them something sweeter than that: both. Usually you have to give up one to get the other. But we're saying: You can have all the freedom you want, and all the income you richly deserved over the past twenty. years or whenever you started. That means we'll have the truly creative people. And if we get the creative people, Marvel or DC can put out 180 books a week, for all I care! If my mom draws them, It don't make no difference anymore.[10]"

It didn’t take long for the house of cards that McFarlane built to come crashing down. As his empire grew, he appeared to forget the basics of what he once preached.

This extended to the way he worked and engaged with people. Seemingly gone was the friendly, inclusive Todd McFarlane, instead replaced by something very strange.

Stephen Bissette recalls, “At one point after the *1963*[11] experience with Image, I was called by Todd McFarlane out of the blue via telephone. He called a few times, always very friendly, chatty, but it was always a bit of a process sorting out what Todd wanted, why he'd called. Initially, it was because Todd wanted me to consider working in some capacity (script, I think) on some *SPAWN*-related horror concept. The conversations were all over the place, but in pursuit of (1) what exactly he wanted me to be doing, and (2) what exactly the 'deal' was, business-wise, my memory is that (1) was an idea he had for a character that was, in essence, a gorilla or oversized simian with a transplanted human brain, and (2) was vague-at-best. Todd really didn't want to nail down what was being offered, or what the 'deal' would be. At one point, he said, ‘Look, if we do something together and I'm happy, I'll take care of you; if you're in my way, I'll flatten you like a steamroller, I'm like an express train and nothing's going to hold me back!’

“I have to say, it wasn't an appealing proposition in either case. Especially after the *1963* experience, in which Jim Valentino was our Image 'Godfather' and had kept everything simple and on the up-and-up with relatively few speed-bumps, I was discouraged with how Jim Lee had abandoned the Annual after seizing its reins at San Diego Comicon 1992, and very wary of further ill-defined anything with anyone at Image, save Jim Valentino (I'd have done anything for/with Jim). I also wasn't excited in the least by the 'transplanted-brain-gorilla' trope, which I'd read in old pulps and comics and seen on TV (*THE MONSTER AND THE GIRL*, 1941) since I was a kid.

“I have no idea what Todd expected of me, and after a final call where I really pressed, politely, for some kind of clear definition of what he wanted and what it paid and what the contract would entail, Todd stopped calling. I reckon he moved on elsewhere, with someone else.

“Somewhere around the same time - 1993-1995, as I was working in earnest on

S.R. Bissette's TYRANT® - I received a phone call from mutual friend Larry Marder, who was working with Todd and the Image circle in various capacities. Todd wanted to see me, wanted to talk to me; again, I'm not sure what about. I also had my friends Tom and Elizabeth Monteleone of Borderlands Press, for whom I'd packaged the first volume of a planned four-volume *From Hell: The Compleat Scripts* (initiated to help earn some income for Alan Moore, sans his having to do additional work, but that's another long story and it ended sadly, due to the movie option contract terminating any such book series existing), which did well, so Tom and Elizabeth asked about maybe my packaging with them the guest scripts from *Spawn* that Alan, Dave Sim, Frank Miller, and Neil Gaiman had written. I was willing to see if such a thing were possible, which would require a conversation with Todd to see if he were interested.

"So, Todd wanted to talk to me about something, and now I had something to approach Todd about, too, on behalf of Borderlands as a publisher and my own imprint, SpiderBaby, as a packager. It so happened that I was going to be visiting the Northwest states, Oregon and Washington, and my friend Diana Schutz wanted to surprise our mutual friends Cam and Isobel Kennedy and their family, who were living for a time up in the Portland area (house swap with someone, I can't recall whom).

"So I timed the trip to visit and stay with Cam and Isobel, and we had a great time; you can fix the time of that trip by the *'Jabba The Hutt'* cover art I did with Cam for one of the Dark Horse comics (my pencils, Cam's inks and colors). I visited the Dark Horse offices in Milwaukie, OR during the trip. Also during that trip, following up on Larry Marder's call, I made arrangements to visit Todd and his wife, and she was as nice as could be, and suggested I bring Cam along with me. So Cam and I made the jaunt over to Todd's studio. When we got there, Todd's wife invited us in and took us upstairs, and she was great; once we got in Todd's studio, though, things were... weird.

"Todd didn't even really say 'hello' to us, though his assistant was attentive and tried to make us comfortable. I was used to "you work when you visit the studio" from my years of friendship with the Mirage Studio guys in Northampton, Massachusetts, and from visiting Dave Sim and Gerhard up in Kitchener, Ontario, so I asked if there was anything I could do - and Todd's assistant handing me a penciled *Spawn* page, a full-page of Spawn in a junk-strewn alley, and I just started inking. Cam sat in the only other available seat, which was right in front of Todd's drawing board - like, right there, in eyeshot of Todd. Todd never made eye contact with either of us, not once. He never spoke to Cam; Todd had this little tray of M&Ms by his board, that he munched on, and he didn't even offer an M&M to Cam.

"It was a weird visit, to say the least. Todd took phone calls, but didn't talk to us, even though the visit had been arranged in order to talk to me, at least. Todd's assistant would try to strike up conversation now and again, but that was increasingly clumsy; Todd's wife came in and offered us something to drink, tea or iced tea, which Cam and I accepted, but from Todd, not a peep - not to US. I finished inking the page, Todd's assistant accepted it from me and whistled in approval, and then we left. Todd was on the phone, we didn't even get a goodbye or a wave. We left, Todd's wife was as charming and courteous as could be, and that was that - but Cam and I were gobsmacked. Cam just couldn't believe it: "He didn't even offer me an M&M," he kept saying. Needless to say, any thought of doing anything with Todd evaporated before I was done inking that page - which you can still see in the respective issue of *Spawn*, and which Todd (or whoever wrote his text pages) acknowledged in the next issue - and that was "all she wrote."

"Sometime after that, I read that Todd and his wife moved to Phoenix, Arizona, I believe. I could say more about what Cam and I saw go down during our brief visit, but the overwhelming impact of just being ignored trumped any and all other impressions. It wasn't like Todd was snooty, or arrogant in our company; it was just like we... didn't exist. Honestly, Cam and I were just flabbergasted.

"Anyhow, that was my last encounter, save for the *Comic Book Rebels* Underwood-Miller signed-and-limited edition experience, in which everyone who agreed to sign except for Todd, signed the signature sheets. That package of signature sheets malingered in Todd's possession for I-don't-remember-how-long, only to be shipped back (in perfect condition) unsigned, so Underwood-Miller just stamped the Todd McFarlane section with some disclaimer, and that was somehow a fitting end to my very peculiar dances - I can't say "with," really, but I guess 'around' Todd.[12]"

The Eclipse Saga

> "There's definitely been a problem getting royalty statements out on time.[1]" – Dean Mullaney

> "Weird doper surfer comic geeks. Too much weed. Low shelf publisher.[2]" – Anonymous creator to author

Eclipse had been one of the forerunners to Image Comics. Founded in 1977 by the Mullaney brothers, Jan and Dean, the company had risen to become one of the more respected independent publishers of the 1980s. Part of Eclipse's business model included the publication of creator owned material. Don McGregor and Paul Gulacy would create one of the first true graphic novels for Eclipse, with their ground-breaking *Sabre: Slow Fade of an Endangered Species* in 1978, years before Marvel released *The Death of Captain Marvel,* a book that Marvel heavily promoted as being the first such book. The brothers added Dean's wife, Cat Yronwode, to the roster and made her a full partner, in charge of editorial.

At their height, Eclipse was publishing comic books featuring work by Chuck Dixon, Norm Breyfogle, P. Craig Russell, Mark Evanier and more. More importantly, the company acquired the rights to reprint, and publish all new material, from Dez Skinn's UK *Warrior* magazine in the form of *Axel Pressbutton* and *Miracleman,* the latter written by Alan Moore. Moore continued the series at Eclipse, and when he finished his storylines, he handed over the reins to Neil Gaiman.

The first cracks in the Eclipse castle began with the treatment of Alan Davis over *Miracleman*. Davis had taken over the art chores from Garry Leach on *Marvelman* in *Warrior*. Under UK copyright laws, Davis had sold the rights for his artwork to be printed in *Warrior* only. When it came to Eclipse Comics, Davis fully intended to hold back permission to reprint his *Marvelman* art due to Alan Moore's refusal to allow Marvel Comics to reprint their seminal *Captain Britain* run. At a time when British writers and artists, such as Brian Bolland, Dave Gibbons and Moore himself, were being courted by American comic book companies, at higher page rates than being offered in the UK, Davis believed that Moore's refusal to allow Marvel USA to reprint *Captain Britain* denied him the opportunity to have his work seen by as many people as possible.

"Initially, I held back my artwork to gain a cut of the copyright because although I was a regular artist on *Marvelman* I wasn't included in the share out of the profits on *Marvelman* merchandising," Alan Davis said in 1989. "It didn't amount to much but it was the principle. I believed the merchandise could only be sold if the characters continued to be popular, and that relied on the continuation of the strip, and I was responsible for that. I was given the copyright and was prepared to resume work on the strip, but problems arose over its syndication. I realized that, since no agreements had been signed and communications between the copyright holders had broken down, it would be better if I put the whole situation down to experience and concentrated on other work.

"The problems over *Marvelman* are the same as those concerning *Captain Britain*! That is, because the ownership of the material is split between the writer and artist, they must both agree on any syndication deal. The *Marvelman* situation is further complicated by the number of copyright holders, so in the past I have been content to go with the flow as long as it promised positive results. However, the recent developments preventing the reprinting of the *Captain Britain* strip angered me so much that I committed the most childish and self-destructive act of my life and refused to allow any of my *Marvelman* work to be reprinted and felt I had no other way of demonstrating the strength of my feelings, even though it meant my actions were as senseless as those I was protesting against. Past experience has taught me that there was no point in trying to talk it over. History is too easily rewritten. My only regret is the amount of people I've offended with my bloody-minded action. I can understand Dean Mullaney's resentment of me; I've made things very difficult for him. But in a way it was inevitable. He came into an ongoing row and accepted one version of the facts that could not be reconciled with the others. I'm so disgusted with the whole affair that I have cut myself free of any future involvement with *Marvelman* by giving my 30% of the copyright to Garry Leach. I'm glad to be rid of it.[3]"

Davis has remained insistent that he was never consulted by Eclipse regarding the reprint, that they published his work illegally and he never received any payments for the American reprints. when it came to the publishing of his work.

Eclipse Comics, via Mullaney and Yronwode, naturally saw things very differently.

"Our most successful title is *Miracleman*, and it has been selling 125,000 copies per month," Dean Mullaney told reporters. "That's generating about $6,000 dollars a month for the creators at 75 cents an issue.[4]"

Cat Yronwode was even more dismissive of Davis. "Dez Skinn signed a contract with Eclipse allowing us to reprint material from *Warrior*, and we intend to reprint that material. If Alan Davis granted Dez Skinn the power to make that contract, and has since changed his mind, that is unfortunate for Alan but he is legally bound to that contract. If Dez Skinn represented himself to Eclipse as having the power to represent Alan Davis when in fact he did not, that is a matter for Alan Davis to settle with Dez Skinn. In any event Eclipse will be reprinting the material.[5]"

Eclipse credited Moore, Davis and Skinn with the copyrights to the contents of *Miracleman* in the first seven issues of the comic. Issue 8, the second issue that had no Alan Davis artwork, saw a trademark notification to both Eclipse and Moore; however, as will be shown, it appears that no such trademark was registered.

The reprints from *Warrior* ceased with issue 7, from there new material would be written by Moore. Faced with no new stories from Quality due to a falling out between Skinn and Moore, Eclipse elected to engage the services of Moore directly. This would see the growing rift between Moore and Davis become irreparable. In his defense, Moore remains adamant that he was duped by

Eclipse when it came to payments, permissions and dealings with Davis.

"They had made certain promises to me that I wanted to be absolutely sure that the artist at that time, Alan Davis, was happy about his work being reprinted. And, I told them that I could not commence writing any new work until they had got that affirmation. They finally left it until the last minute, and then asked me why I hadn't got the new *Marvelman* work in, at which point I reiterated my request for some proof that Alan Davis was okay about the whole thing. They said that they were getting this proof - and that they really needed me to start work - that this proof existed, that it was on its way, and they would be showing it to me as soon as possible. I started work because I believed that they were telling the truth. I later found out this was not the case. So, by the time I'd finished working with *Marvelman*, I was pretty sick of all the publishers that had been involved with it up to that point.[6]"

As Moore continued to write the title Davis grew angrier about what he perceived as a betrayal by all concerned.

"When I first read the above, I felt really sad that Alan's work had been so badly impaired by deep concern over the legality of Eclipse publishing MY art. He was so distraught in fact, that he must have forgotten he had my address and telephone number, or if he was too nervous to call, could have contacted me via a mutual acquaintance, like Jamie Delano, rather than suffer such creatively debilitating doubts. But I suppose Alan's recollection, for what it's worth, proves my case. The reason Eclipse could not furnish the proof Alan required to commence work is because it didn't exist. They, Eclipse, knew I had withheld my permission to have my work reprinted.[7]"

By 1986 Skinn and Leach washed their hands of their portions of *Miracleman* and reportedly sold them to Eclipse for $8,000. Again, Davis was not consulted about the sale, let alone paid. Moore worked with *Swamp Thing* collaborators Rick Veitch and John Totleben for the remainder of his *Miracleman* run.

Moore remained with the title until issue 16 after which he handed over authorship, along with his share in *Miracleman*, to Neil Gaiman. Gaiman signed a contract calling for a payment of $60 per page with royalties to come into effect if a single issue sold in excess of 50,000 copies. He began work with artist Mark Buckingham.

A schedule was also amended to the contract. The schedule called for scripts to be delivered the following issues on the relevant dates. It was a good schedule, but, ultimately, one that would never be met. In the first instance, only eight issues would be published. Below is a breakdown of the issues published, with their original scheduled script dates.

17 - April 15, 1989 – published June 1990

18 - May 15 1 1989– published August 1990

19 - July 15, 1989– published November 1990

20 - August 15, 1989– published March 1991

21 - October 15, 1989– published July 1991

22 - December 15, 1989– published August 1991

23 - January 15, 1990– published June 1992

24 - February 15, 1990– published June 1993

None of the following issues were ever published by Eclipse but remained on the schedule (with their original scheduled dates listed).

25 - March 15, 1990

26 - April 15, 1990

27 - May 15, 1990

28 - July 15, 1990

29 - August 15, 1990

30 - October 15, 1990

31 - December 15, 1990

32 - January 15, 1991

33 - February 15, 1991

34 - March 15, 1991

The beginning of the end for Eclipse came when Toren Smith decided to sue for payment. Smith had handled the translation and packaging of Eclipse's line of Japanese comic reprints, *Appleseed, Black Magic, Dominion, Cyber 7, Dirty Pair, What's Michael,* and *Lost Continent* via his Studio Proteus. Erratic payments saw him take the Japanese comics to Dark Horse where he discovered that Eclipse had been underpaying him. He subsequently asked for an audit, which showed the discrepancy. "Eclipse has been paying late for the last three years," Smith told the Comics Journal. "Their accountings have been peculiar, and I am now taking legal steps on behalf of myself and the Japanese to get what we're owed.[8]"

Toren Smith was looking for a total of $150,561 for payments due and at least $1,000,000 in damages. Ultimately winning the suit, the court awarded him $122,328. This was the end for Eclipse as any monies that came into the company would be deposited into an escrow account and handed directly to Smith. This now meant that no creator could be paid any royalty, and, with no further income being available to the company, it appeared that it would have no option other than to fold.

When it came to issuing payments, Cat Yronwode denied any responsibility, and placed all the blame squarely onto Dean Mullaney. "In the entire time I've been associated with Eclipse I've never been permitted to write checks or see the books of the company," she said. "I only deal with the editorial department. The only monetary stuff I oversee is the warehouse.[9]"

In return Dean Mullaney placed the blame for missing payments squarely at the feet of his brother Jan. "It's been Jan's responsibility to send out royalty statements and that he hadn't had the time to do it," Dean said. "That's the main reason why I'm taking over that job to make sure people get their royalty statements on time.[10]"

In the midst of the turmoil, Mullaney and Yronwode split and ultimately divorced. Both parties have different views upon the impact that their split had upon Eclipse.

"What happened at the very end," Yronwode would say, "was that Dean essentially abandoned Eclipse when he abandoned me.[11]"

"I've never really told anyone why Eclipse folded," Mullaney said in 2005. "It had nothing to do with Cat and I getting divorced. We entered into a co-publishing deal with HarperCollins. It was an exclusive deal both ways. In the beginning, it was a fantastic relationship. We did all the production and were invited to give presentations at all their sales meetings in the US and UK. They made fantastic floor and counter displays for bookstores. When they released *The Hobbit* graphic novel, they sold more copies in the UK alone than Ballantine did in all the US! The problems started when we asked for sales figures on the other books (*Miracleman*, Clive Barker's titles, *Dragonflight*, Dean Koontz's *Trapped*, etc.). We never received a single sales statement. Therefore, no royalty statements. So there I was paying advances to creators, tying up all my capital. And then nothing from Harper. No statements, no money. Meanwhile, creators were naturally asking for their statements and royalties. I explained the situation, but still never got anything from Harper. It got to the point that I had no cash left to even carry on normal business because we had laid out everything we had for advances. All that was left to do was sell off every piece of inventory I could get my hands on, pay all the little guys (individual creators and small vendors), and stiff the large ones (printers and freight companies). And declare bankruptcy.[12]"

David Campiti was the co-owner of Glass House Graphics and acted as the agent for artist Mike Deodato Jr, amongst others. Campiti was also chasing Eclipse for payment of $20,000 for work that Deodato had done on a proposed, but never published, book *Miracleman: Triumphant*.

"We were doing a ton of work for Eclipse," Campiti told The Comics Journal. "The Barker stuff, a monthly *Miracleman* spin-off by Mike Deodato, Dean was having me arrange a license for *Die Hard*. Then everything fell apart - money stopped coming, royalties were nowhere to be seen, I was being told Dean had separated from and was divorcing Cat, he was moving to New York. He was conveniently avoiding phone calls and faxes. Once in a blue moon I would get a fax dealing with maybe ten percent of the things I was asking about, and even then, the answers were so full of holes you could drive a starship through them.[13]"

Unlike Smith, the amount owed to Campiti was not of sufficient value to sue. "My lawyer tells me that if Eclipse is so low on funds there's not a lot I can do. If I go the route of Toren Smith, I could spend twice as much in legal fees as I intend to collect. I don't have 40 grand to spend to collect 20.[14]"

Unfortunately for Campiti, Mullaney was now reduced to the traditional 'the check's in the mail' routine. This only served to anger Campiti more, who then contacted HarperCollins and after speaking to Managing Director Malcolm

Edwards, discovered that what Mullaney had been telling him might not have been totally accurate.

"Edwards was outlining a very interesting story where HarperCollins had apparently paid Dean for most of the stuff I was asking about, according to their records. They faxed me the itemized total for what they had paid Dean, and it had included work that GHG had not done. This implies two possibilities: there had been other work done on the book which we knew nothing about either before or after we started it, or Dean had vouchered for more than we had turned in. I don't know which is the case, because Dean isn't forthcoming with answers, but I have an opinion as to which is the real scenario. I can believe that if there was some difficulty as perceived by HC on the part of Eclipse's follow-through, which I've certainly seen at my end, and if HarperCollins saw a problem - books coming out late, Eclipse's bookkeeping being extremely shoddy, they might think, 'Whoa, maybe this isn't a good idea, let's slow down.'[15]"

After dodging a meeting with Campiti at Philadelphia (where he allegedly used the 'cheque in the mail excuse'), Campiti was keen to get to Dean Mullaney at the San Diego Comic Con. Mullaney promised Campiti that he would be there and would meet him. In the meantime, although he was crying poor, Mullaney had moved from New York to Florida.

"There were two bank accounts, one in New York and one here in Forestville, California," Yronwode recalled. "I could not sign checks on the New York account, but on the Forestville account, Dean had signature power, and so did I. Dean cleared out the Forestville bank account long distance, from New York, and there was no money to pay David Campiti. I was at the San Diego Convention that year and Dean did not show up. He had run off with his new lover, and I was trying to hold together a booth showcasing twenty-seven new products we had just come out with since he left. In addition to dealing with my husband leaving me after twelve years, this was pretty dramatic for me because Campiti had been told by Dean to bring artwork and there was no money![16]"

"The last time I talked to Dean on the phone, he was trying to set up some kind of meeting in San Diego," Campiti recalled. "I replied, 'Gee, this smacks of exactly the way you handled things last October in Philadelphia.' I poked holes into what he said. I told him I was interested in seeing how a man like him can sleep nights. I set up a time to meet him; he didn't show up. Late on Wednesday at the end of the trade show prior to the convention, I spotted him. I ran out to get him, and he said, 'I can't talk to you; I need to get to the airport.' I responded, 'We need to talk. You promised we'd talk. You owe me money; we have a lot of things to go over.' He insisted he had to get to the airport, so I said, 'Fine, I'll go to the airport with you and we can talk while you wait for your plane.' His face turned white. We're walking toward the front of the convention center; he's a good foot taller than I am, he's walking at his top stride, and I'm trying to keep up with him. We get outside and he turns and says, 'I'll give you one minute. What?' I asked him two questions, and he gives me answers that are full of baloney. I said, 'Dean, why are you lying?' He looked around and said, 'I can't deal with this,' and he ran. Literally. I haven't spoken to him since. I'm increasing my phone bills without getting my artists paid. This is not a good situation. I find it fascinating that a man who can't even cut a $10 check can afford to move to Florida.[17]"

Eclipse also owed Gaiman and Buckingham for their work on *Miracleman*, to the point where neither man would begin work on an issue until they had been paid for the previous one. The non-payment for *Miracleman* extended back to the very first issue.

"I got paid two, maybe three royalty statements in my four and half, five years working with them," Gaiman told The Comics Journal "And each time it would begin with me sending faxes and end with grumpy upsets on their part, and eventually I would get a check out of them. I haven't spoken to Dean since the very beginning of this year. I think that what is symptomatic of the Toren Smith case is symptomatic of what happened with Miracleman basically, there's some very, very creative accountancy going on with no royalties being paid unless they have to be.

"Alan Moore hasn't been paid any royalties since #1; Mark is owed for at least the last issue, #25. As far as I can tell, none of the artists have been paid any royalties: Gary Leach, Alan Davis, Rick Veitch, John Totleben, Chuck Beckum.[18]"

However, in a response to this statement, artist Rick Veitch confirmed that he indeed was paid for his work, and was paid royalties for the paperback reprints of his work from Eclipse. However no royalties were paid for the hardcovers[19].

Gaiman and Buckingham had finished *Miracleman* #25, but it was never published. Fortunately, Gaiman was able to retrieve the art.

"They had the art, but I don't think they had the money to color it and I don't think they had the money to print it, either. So it was sitting in a drawer and Cat phoned me. I said, 'Look, I'm getting really concerned given some of the weirder stuff Dean is doing to make money that I will turn around one day and see that *Miracleman* #25 is appearing in Playboy Comics as a one-shot since none of us are getting paid.' And she said that this was a valid and serious concern, 'Would you like the art back?' and I said, 'Yes, I would,' because stuff was disappearing. So Cat – good call, bless her heart – she sent us the art back.[20]"

Dez Skinn was also having troubles getting money owed from Eclipse, leading to Eclipse to stop using film provided from Skinn and instead using photocopies of old *Warrior* magazines in an attempt to circumvent payments. Skinn, who had a contract with Eclipse, hounded the company to the point where he met Jan Mullaney, "in New York, in some really seedy bar. He turned up looking like a real hippie with a couple of thousand dollars in cash in a brown envelope.[21]"

The cash in a brown bag worked and Skinn resumed business with Eclipse for the time being.

Mullaney tried to find a way out though. After paying a reported $20,000, Eclipse offered Toren Smith *Miracleman* instead of the outstanding money. Smith, after consulting Gaiman, declined the offer.

It was at this point in 1994 that questions were asked about the ownership of *Miracleman*. "The legal situation is a far bigger can of worms than anyone ever thought," Gaiman told The Comics Journal. "As I understand it, when *Miracleman* was originally revived in *Warrior* as *Marvelman*, Dez Skinn, the publisher at the time, claimed he had bought the character from the Official Receiver, which in England is the area of the government which handles bankruptcy. Apparently *Miracleman* was the property of a long bankrupt publisher. That was what Skinn had told Alan Moore and Dean Mullaney at the time. This appears to have proved false, and Dez no longer claims this; he now just sort of claims he found it lying around or something. Eclipse has signed documents from Skinn affirming that Dez owns the character, that Dez had officially bought the character and was selling Eclipse his share. Mark Buckingham and I have essentially Alan Moore's share of the character, which we obtained when we started doing it. So what is *Miracleman* worth? It seems to sort of be worth rubbles. There are a lot of publishers who would have wanted to take over *Miracleman*, but it is such a can of worms. It would be a natural for Vertigo, but in order to take over *Miracleman*... you have to straighten out a number of things which have been, if not unethical, then at least questionable on the part of Eclipse's past business practices - like making sure that Alan Davis and company are taken care of.[22]"

"That's accurate as far as I can remember," Alan Moore told the same magazine. "I never saw any royalties from *Miracleman*, and from what I hear it was one of their bestselling books.[23]"

In February 1986, the Russian River, which runs through Sonoma County in California, was swelling from an unprecedented rain period. A storm had swept through the county depositing upwards of twenty inches into the river, causing an inland tsunami. The river burst its banks as the wave of muddy water made its way down to the ocean. In Guerneville, rain kept falling as the river came through and it crested at just less than 49 feet, a record that still stands. People lost their lives in the sudden flood, buildings and property were destroyed and hundreds were made homeless.

One of the houses flooded belonged to Dean Mullany and Cat Yronwode. Literally everything they had, other than those few items stored in their attic, which was, luckily, just above the high-water mark, was destroyed forever. This included an unknown quantity of Eclipse comic books, along with the company's records, original art, negatives, film, stats and much more. One of the titles affected was *Miracleman.* Issue 8 of the Eclipse *Miracleman* was a fill-in, as Mullaney and Yronwode were battling to rebuild their lives.

Yronwode recalled the flood with dramatics. "It all started with some rain; you see. A little bit more rain than we usually get up here in northern California. To tell the truth, it turned out to be a hell of a lot of rain, and it didn't have anywhere to go but downhill. Downhill, in this case, meant our house, our office, our town – in fact, the western half of our entire county.

"We all got out with our lives, but not much else. Sean Deming (our stalwart assistant editor), Dean Mullaney, and yours truly had to watch as just about everything we owned went under the rising waters. The Eclipse office, located on the second floor of a downtown building, only took in a couple of feet of misplaced and muddied raindrops. We had to get evacuated by helicopters. We lost all our back-issue comics and most of the film negatives used to reprint the stuff overseas.[24]"

It is possible that the film, and other physical assets, for the first seven issues of *Miracleman* do not exist, and that they were wiped out in the Guerneville flood along other the pre-1986 Eclipse comics.

Such an explanation appears to be too simplistic and it discounts Gaiman's claim, and Mullaney's admissions, that large portions of *Miracleman* were sold prior to the 1996 bankruptcy auction. A more likely answer is that Dean Mullaney sold the *Miracleman* assets to a purchaser in Canada, who wasn't Todd McFarlane. In all likeliness, that person was Roger Broughton.

Eclipse: Bankrupt & Sold

As a result of the Toren Smith judgement, in combination with the divorce, monies owing to creators such as Gaiman, Buckingham, Deodato, Skinn, Moore, Davis, Leach, the flood and dwindling sales, Eclipse folded and filed for Chapter 7 bankruptcy in 1995.

> "Chapter 7 bankruptcy is the simplest and most common form of bankruptcy. In Chapter 7, if the debtor has assets not protected by an exemption, a court appointed trustee may sell the assets and distribute the net proceeds to creditors according to the priorities established in the Code." (Moran Law Group).

Amazingly, although he was the principle, contracted writer on the company's flagship title, nobody told Gaiman, Buckingham, Skinn or anyone else for that matter that Eclipse had folded.

This brings us to the question of what happened to the back stock of comic books, trading cards and books that Eclipse once had?

The answer to that is simple. While it's true that McFarlane got some of it, it was only a drop in the ocean of what was once owned by Eclipse. The reason why there was so little for McFarlane was simple – the bulk of it had been thrown out and/or held back from the bankruptcy sale.

Again, Yronwode placed blame at the feet of Mullaney. "At the time of the bankruptcy, Dean Mullaney, who was the publisher, sold most of the warehouse stock to a dealer in remainders, but he did not clean out the warehouse. He told a local handyman to take everything to the dump. I decided that was a silly thing to do, so I paid for one month more storage on the warehouse and then cleaned the warehouse out.[1]"

As noted previously, Mullaney was busily selling off as many of the Eclipse assets to whoever would pay, however, by all accounts; he was doing this *before* the company was placed into bankruptcy. Yronwode, in her own words, was selling off the stock *after* the company was placed into bankruptcy. The main purchaser was Bud Plant, who had a rule when it came to purchasing Eclipse stock – he would only buy unopened boxes of books and comics.

"As far as I know, he might be sitting on an entire warehouse of that stuff," Yronwode declared. "He would not take any case that was opened. So he left a tremendous amount of material - all random. And we had subscription fulfillment boxes. I got all of that by cleaning out the warehouse.[2]"

Yronwode didn't declare the stock that she had in her possession to the Chapter 7 bankruptcy trustee, electing instead to hold it back and sell it herself. "I didn't even bother to raise prices, as the comics became more desirable. I did it because the former office manager of Eclipse, Susie Bosselmann, needed a job. I set up the Comics Warehouse to keep her in money. She got all of the proceeds, and I went to work for Claypool Comics.[3]"

There are issues with these statements. First and foremost is the statement that Yronwode sold off subscription stock. These are comics that have already been bought and paid for by the general public. By not sending those comics out to the people who had paid subscriptions, Yronwode effectively took money under false pretenses. No matter the intentions, as good as they might have been (paying Bosselmann for her work), what happened went against the rules of bankruptcy.

Eclipse Comics was placed into Chapter 7 bankruptcy. Under the rules of Chapter 7 all the remaining assets of the company were to be handed over to the official trustee to sell to pay the remaining bills. Clearly this was not done. Official declarations have been sworn, and failure to answer truthfully, even by omission, amounts to perjury.

There are ramifications to withholding property under Chapter 7 bankruptcy.

> If you fail to list some of your assets or property on your bankruptcy papers and the trustee finds out, here's what might happen.
>
> **You won't be able to discharge your debts**. If you hide assets from the bankruptcy court, you won't be entitled to receive a discharge (the order that wipes out qualifying debt) and will continue to owe all of the debt that you were trying to get rid of in bankruptcy. But your case won't be dismissed in Chapter 7 bankruptcy. The property you're not allowed to keep (exempt) under the law will still have to be turned over to the trustee assigned to your case and sold to pay your creditors. You'll continue to owe any amount not paid through the bankruptcy.
>
> **The trustee can revoke your discharge**. If the trustee finds hidden assets, the trustee can ask the court to revoke or take back your discharge. The trustee can do this at any time before the case closes or, even after, up to one year after the discharge date. (Learn more in What Happens If My Bankruptcy Discharge Is Revoked?)
>
> **You cannot discharge those debts in subsequent bankruptcies**. The debts that you list in any bankruptcy where your discharge was denied or revoked for hiding assets cannot be discharged in a subsequent bankruptcy filing.
>
> **You could face criminal charges**. You sign your bankruptcy schedules listing your assets under penalty of perjury, representing that they are true and accurate. The penalty for bankruptcy fraud is a fine of up to $250,000, imprisonment for up to twenty years, or both[4].

The three owners of Eclipse, Jan and Dean Mullaney and Cat Yronwode, would have been made aware of their legal obligations at the time of filing for bankruptcy, so there would have been no excuse for a failure to declare the Eclipse assets. The statements since, from Yronwode in 2002 and Mullaney in 2005, show that they deliberately hid assets from the trustee for their own reasons, along with selling off subscription stock that should have been sent out to those who had already paid.

The results of the Chapter 7 bankruptcy saw Eclipse's physical and intellectual assets put up for auction. There wasn't much left of Eclipse as Dean Mullaney had been busily selling anything he could.

As Gaiman said, when discussing the physical assets that McFarlane had sent him in 1997, "It wasn't the complete set of *Miracleman* film. I received a phone call from Terry Fitzgerald either when he sent it off or when I got it saying that some of the film had been illicitly sold under the counter by the former owner of Eclipse to some guy in Toronto who was trying to hold Todd up for it and they didn't have that stuff.[5]"

In his attempts to make sure people got paid, Mullaney had gutted the Eclipse assets to the point where what remained was largely meaningless, other than the *Miracleman* trademark.

> PLEASE TAKE NOTICE that the undersigned Trustee will sell at public auction through Henry A Leonard & Co. on February 29, 1996 at 11:00 a.m., those assets belonging to the debtor and located at the Willowcove Marina, 9 Hudson Drive in Stony Point, New York. The auctioneer will sell all of the Trustee's right, title and interest, if any, in and to the following assets (subject to all liens, if any), in and to the following property:
>
> *Copyrights, trademarks, characters and other intellectual property, miscellaneous film negatives and color separations, publishing agreements with any authors, illustrators and other rights holders, in connection with various comic book series, miscellaneous comic books and cards.* (Notice of Intended Sale, 2 February 1996)

"It was a bankruptcy sale," said Terry Fitzgerald. "It was whatever was included in the bankruptcy sale of the Eclipse. It was a live auction that was done over the phone and I was bidding on behalf of TMP. Physically I don't I don't know if the location was at Eclipse comics or some bankruptcy holding. Todd wanted to expand our catalog of characters. Eclipse had several different characters that were attached to it. *Black Terror* is one. *Air Boy* would be another. *Miracleman.* I talked to Dean Mullaney. I don't specifically remember about what. It would have been more about the sale and whether or not what was listed on the inventory was correct.[6]"

The Notice of Intended Sale was sent to everyone who had worked for, or dealt with, Eclipse. For many this was the first notification they had that Eclipse had folded. That list included *Miracleman* creators Alan Moore, Garry Leach and Alan Davis, *Batman* co-creator Bob Kane, Clive Barker, agent Glenn Lord, actress Jewel Shepard, David Wenzel, Dreamworks and Harper Collins, along with Jan Mullaney and Cat Yronwode and several others. Word quickly spread that the Eclipse copyrights and trademarks were up for auction and before long several interested parties began sniffing around. One of those people was Todd McFarlane.

For most of the interested parties, the jewel in the crown was *Miracleman.* The character, along with the potential of obtaining reprint rights to works by Alan Moore, Alan Davis, Garry Leach, Rick Veitch, John Totleben, Neil Gaiman, Mark Buckingham and others who had worked on the title interested people more than anything else.

The first offer for *Miracleman* came in late October, 1995, when a firm named Marlow & Company, made an offer of $2,380 for the following: "Copyrights, trademarks, characters and other intellectual property, film negatives and color separations, related to and comprising the *Miracleman* comic book series and publishing agreements with any authors, illustrators and other rights holders in connection with the *Miracleman* comic book series." After consulting with Mullaney, the bankruptcy Trustee rejected the offer, instead deciding to send *Miracleman* to the auction block in the hopes of making as much money as possible. Dean Mullaney had already been making money out of the sale of *Miracleman* assets and there was the rejected offer from Toren Smith to bear in mind, which amounted to, potentially, $80,000 in an open auction.

Without *Miracleman* the Eclipse assets were heavily diluted. What also wasn't considered was the so called $80,000 offer was one made to Toren Smith by Mullaney and, ultimately, not accepted.

The auction took place on 29 February 1996. Eight interested parties were present at the allocated time, 11:00am, either in person or via phone, but nobody actually got a chance to bid. Those who did call at the appointed time were quickly told that the auction was over before it began, and that an offer had been accepted. That offer was $25,000, cash, for all of Eclipses' remaining assets, including inventory, copyrights and trademarks. The offer had been submitted via telephone by Terry Fitzgerald, acting on behalf of Todd McFarlane. After the offer was formally accepted Eclipse Comics now belonged to Todd

McFarlane Productions.

McFarlane was clear from the start, he only wanted *Miracleman* but wasn't baulking from owning the remaining assets of Eclipse.

"At the last minute, I found out that you had to buy the whole company to get any of the pieces," McFarlane told The Comics Journal. "Also, knowing some of the people who had ties to Eclipse made me comfortable with it. I employ Beau Smith, who worked there a lot, and Larry Marder had some past experiences there. Until I get it all sorted out and see what I have got on my table I just felt better that a guy like me buy it. If I decide to do nothing I can afford to put it off in a corner and not really damage it, as opposed to some of the other people there who I just thought were kind of fly by night people. Everybody wanted to piecemeal this thing. That's where my interest was originally but now I am not interested in selling off a piece here and a piece there. I now own a company I wasn't expecting to own. I think I am in a lot better position to do something with it than some stupid little start-up company. I just have to make a plan of attack and do it, but I am in no hurry. It's not like I need another company that bad.[7]"

Another reason why McFarlane bought Eclipse was quickly circulated. In 1993 McFarlane had done a licensing deal with Eclipse for the latter to produce a set of *Spawn Spogz*. These pogs were, to that point, the only non-Image, non-McFarlane controlled *Spawn* item in the marketplace. By buying Eclipse, McFarlane was assured of retaining complete and utter ownership of his *Spawn* universe.

Contacted immediately after the auction, McFarlane was positive about the future of *Miracleman*. "This is in Neil's court right now. We talk on a semi-regular basis and I am sure that when we both get out from under our workloads, we will actually figure out what to do with it. This could be a hot potato. If they (Gaiman and Buckingham) don't want it, it's a cold potato, and if they do want to do it, it's a hot potato. If I was to go and do *Miracleman*, it is my duty to offer it to them, and if they refuse then my duty is done.[8]"

From the start there were warning signs that McFarlane might not have bought *Miracleman*. As part of the sale, McFarlane was informed, via letter, that he was obligated to check on the status of ownership of the characters that he had bought, as the trademarks might not be free and clear. The letter also makes it clear that the current ownership of the characters had been discussed with Terry Fitzgerald, and, presumably, McFarlane.

> "As discussed, I have enclosed a copy of various documents supplied by one of the principals of Eclipse. He also advised me that Eclipse has a trademark in *New Wave* and that for the characters that it does not own, namely *New Wave* and *Airboy*, that it had publishing agreements with the creators. The Trustee cannot confirm this and does not make any representation as to the accuracy of same. As discussed, the onus is on you.as purchaser, to do your due diligence investigation.[9]"

It was advice that McFarlane appears to have ignored. As can be seen from the following exchange, McFarlane appeared to only be interested in obtaining trademarks and copyrights, not the physical stock (which included boxes of *Miracleman* trade paperbacks along with single issues), of Eclipse, and, six years after buying the assets, he believed that he had bought those rights free and clear.

"There's a company called Eclipse comics that published a lot of comic books," McFarlane told the courts in 2002. "They must have must have had some financial difficulties because at some point they went into bankruptcy and within the confines of it going into bankruptcy some of the books and the properties that they had in the past were part of what the assets were that you would potentially be adding on in that bankruptcy hearing or auction or I don't even know what it officially was called. And within the confines of that then in talking about Terry Fitzgerald, you know, I went, "Hey, Eclipse is up. You know, there's some cool characters in there. You know, we should sort of stick our nose in and see -- see what sort of comes out of it. I think they held a telephone auction. A handful of people were on it. I don't believe they ID'd anybody. And just to make sure they didn't, I think I even had Terry doing the bidding for me so they didn't think big Daddy Warbucks is here. And so there was a sort of a quick, fairly quick auction and I ended up winning the auction and all of the provisions that came with it through the bankruptcy trustee that was presiding over it.

"Physically it was like some reprints of comic books or inventory of comic books. I think there was some trading cards. There may have been a little bit of film. Just sort of knickknacks. I think they were just sort of clearing out Eclipse's warehouse and whatever had dust on it that sort of went, the whole kit and kaboodle at that point. Then the intellectual properties that went with it, the trademarks and properties that went with the auction that they said there were trademarks and copyrights to some of the characters that went with it. So those were sort of more interesting to me than back issues of books that nobody cared about.[10]"

As has been reported earlier, the warehouse that McFarlane talked about had been cleared out by Yronwode and Mullaney well before the bankruptcy agents got to it.

"Todd first mentioned *Miracleman* to me when he bought the Eclipse assets," Gaiman would recall, "which I think was either some month earlier than that because he had phoned me up and asked if I knew anything about some Canadian guy who was trying to buy *Miracleman* alone and if I knew anything about this. I said yes, the guy had gotten in touch with me and asked if Mark Buckingham and I would be willing to continue with *Miracleman* if he got the rights. And I said sure, you know, we wanted to get on with it, good luck in the auction, but he never sent me any of that film or anything like that. Todd said that he was thinking of bidding on the whole of Eclipse or that he had just bid on the whole of Eclipse. Terry Fitzgerald phoned me up and wanted to know what I knew about something called *Miracleman Triumphant*, which was some kind of series that Eclipse had been doing toward the end of Eclipse. I was never clear whether he had any of the artwork for it or not.[11]"

It appears that McFarlane didn't buy any artwork, or film, for *Miracleman Triumphant*. *Miracleman Triumphant* was a Gaiman approved spin-off series that was to be written by Fred Burke and illustrated by Mike Deodato Jr and Jason Temujin Minor. The first issue had been completed and the second in the works when Eclipse collapsed. What happened to that art remains a mystery.

"All along, Eclipse had attempted to create other *Miracleman* titles to help them exploit the perceived potential of the property," wrote Pádraig Ó Méalóid. "Besides the *Miracleman*: *Apocrypha* series they were also planning a series called *Miracleman: Triumphant* which, according to Yronwode, was to have been plotted and co-edited by Gaiman (although he claims to have no knowledge of this), and which would fill in the ten-year gap between the last events in Moore's story and Gaiman's story starting. This was to be written by Eclipse editor Fred Burke and drawn by Mike Deodato Jr, but never actually came about, although one issue was written and drawn up, apparently, and ads for it appeared in some issues of *Miracleman.*[12]"

"How odd that Neil Gaiman "claims to have no knowledge" of the "*Miracleman Triumphant*" mini-series by Fred Burke and Mike Deodato, Jr," Cat Yronwode posted on line. "I certainly recall our having an editorial discussion by phone about this proposed "continuity implant" and I recall us working out a storyline that would not interfere with anything he had planned. Shortly thereafter, Fred, Mike, and I were given the go-ahead by Jan and Dean to start the work. Later, when Eclipse was falling apart, I called Gaiman, among other creators, to arrange the return of material (which he has acknowledged that I did) - and at that time I asked him what he wanted me to do about the "*Miracleman Triumphant*" art, as I figured he was somehow a co-owner of it, and might find a new publisher for the series. He told me that he didn't want it sent to him as he had not directly worked on it. So I didn't send it to him. He certainly knew it existed, even though he has forgotten it now.[13]"

So, exactly what did Todd McFarlane get for his $25,000?

That can be answered by looking at the inventory list provided to him at the time. In summary McFarlane got multiple copies of the following comic books: *Velocity, Hobbit, Parts Unknown, David Chelsea In Love, Eclipse, Parts Unknown, Target Airboy, I Saw It, Clive Barker's Tapping The Vein, Airboy, Miracleman* and *Miracleman Apocrypha,* plus several trade paperbacks of *Miracleman*. He got 13 copies of Bob Kane's autobiography, *Batman and Me*. Trading cards included sets, packets and entire boxes of *Friendly Dictator, Foul Baseball, Bush League, Crime & Punishment, National Lampoon Loaded Weapon* and *Famous Comic Creators.*

As for the film, art and stats, this is where things get interesting. For *Miracleman*, McFarlane received covers and film for issues 6, 7, 8, 15, 21 and 23. There was partial film, damaged, for *Miracleman 3D*. He received covers for issues 1, 2, 4, 13, 17, 18, 19 and 20. There were color keys for issue 21. And film for *Miracleman: Man of Dreams, Exiled Gods* and *Miracleman Family.*

McFarlane also bought covers and film for issues of *Tapping The Vein, Valkyrie, Black Terror* and *Airboy.*

On a whole the true value of the sale lay in the trademarks and contracts that were sold. The comics were of minor value. Added up, without knowing how many were in the boxes that are just listed as 'box' McFarlane bought a couple of thousand issues of what can be best described as filler stock. The film and covers were incomplete for all the titles listed.

According to John Jackson Miller, Eclipse published 233 unique titles from 1985 onwards. "As you can see, Capital's files didn't include many Eclipse books - generally short-run titles or any comics released before 1985. Most everything that was reported was a better-seller, with sales of at least 1,500 copies. The longest-running title with no data reported was Xenon, a Viz/Eclipse hybrid anime book, at 23 issues long. Since the higher profile books have sales data, you might figure that the reporting titles would have probably sold as well as the two-thirds of no-data titles combined - figure 5 million copies total through Capital, all-time. Then it's just a matter of what we think Capital's market share of Eclipse titles would be. If you think it's one-third, for example, then the total universe would be 15 million copies. But there are a lot of assumptions in there, no matter what you do.[14]"

Adding in known pre-1985 titles the list reaches 269 unique titles. This includes one-shot issues. They published, post-1985, 1,223 unique issues that were recorded. If there were 15,000,000 comic books sold, then there would have been at least a third of that that went unsold, accounting for perhaps 5,000,000 individual comic books. Even accounting for the Guerneville flood, which happened in 1986, then there should have been a lot, lot more than what McFarlane received. Only 26 of these titles were represented, it remains to be known what happened to the film, and stock, of the other 90% of the company's output.

Missing were film, negatives, stats and separations, along with the comic books, to properties by Jack Kirby and Steve Gerber (*Destroyer Duck*), P. Craig Russell, Bernie Wrightson, Clive Barker, Chris Ware, Don McGregor, Gene Colan, Marshall Rogers, Trina Robbins, Steve Niles, Brian Bolland, Alex Toth, Eddie Campbell, Mark Evanier, Fred Hembeck, Tim Truman, Kurt Busiek, Terry Beatty, Max Allen Collins, Scott McCloud, Michael T Gilbert, Chuck Dixon, Frank Brunner, Bruce Jones, John Bolton and many more.

Also missing were copyrights to any material that Eclipse had published. While a copyright is naturally assigned to any published work the moment it appears, there is a provision in American copyright law for a copyright to be registered and assigned to a person or a company. Despite the output of Eclipse, the company, Eclipse Comics, owned very few actual copyrights. These copyrights consisted of the following:

Airboy and Mr. Monster Special #1: shared with Michael T Gilbert and Mark Pacella

Crossfire and Rainbow issues 1 to 4: shared with Mark Evanier, Will Meugniot and Dan Spiegle

Doc Stearn-Mister Monster issues 1 to 8: shared with Michael T Gilbert

The Heroine: shared with James Brock Jr

Miracleman issues 17 to 23: shared with Neil Gaiman and Mark Buckingham. These were the only issues of *Miracleman* that Eclipse Comics registered a copyright for.

Nada: shared with Rodeo Suplex Inc.

The New DNAgents issues 1 to 17: shared with Mark Evanier and Will Meugniot

This did not mean that these copyrights were the property of Eclipse Comics even though they had been registered with the US Copyright Office. No other IP had been registered under the name of Eclipse Comics.

So why did Eclipse register these comics, and not others? More than likely it was just routine as Cat Yronwode was, correctly it must be noted, registering copyrights for her work in Timothy Truman's *Scout* and Will Eisner's *The Spirit* under her own name at roughly the same time.

> "Registration is recommended for a number of reasons. Many choose to register their works because they wish to have the facts of their copyright on the public record and have a certificate of registration. Registered works may be eligible for statutory damages and attorney's fees in successful litigation.[15]"

Who owns these copyrights now?

Not Todd McFarlane. Copyrights, like any other property, can be transferred by the owner to another person, company or parties. This can be a partial copyright or the entire work, but the transfer is not as simple as merely buying a business name.

"Any or all of the copyright owner's exclusive rights, or parts of those rights, can be transferred. The transfer, however, generally must be made in writing and signed by the owner of the rights conveyed or the owner's authorized agent. Transferring a right on a nonexclusive basis does not require a written agreement. You can bequeath a copyright by will or pass it along as personal property under applicable state laws of intestate succession. It can also be conveyed by operation of law. You can 'record' a transfer of copyright ownership with the Copyright Office through its Office of Public Records and Repositories. Although recordation is not required to make a valid transfer between parties, it does provide certain legal advantages.[16]"

If McFarlane did buy copyrights from Eclipse, they were for partial works and, sadly, the transfer, to this point, has not been recorded. The copyrights to the works noted belong to the creators named, notably Mark Evanier, Michael T Gilbert, Neil Gaiman, Mark Buckingham, Will Meugniot, Mark Pacella and Dan Spiegle. McFarlane can't do anything with the work, but those who have the copyright most certainly can. For the record, *DNAgents* was trademarked to Meugniot and Evanier but was cancelled as of 1992 and *Doc Sterrn...Mr. Monster* is trademarked to Michael T Gilbert. The other works were never trademarked.

With regards to trademarks McFarlane bought the rights to the name Eclipse Comics (registered July 21, 1987), along with *Airboy* (REGISTERED July 28, 1987). The bill of sale clearly indicates that he did not buy *Miracleman.* In 1996, what McFarlane thought was the *Miracleman* trademark, as presented in the sale, actually wasn't.

So, in 1996, who owned *Miracleman*?

Cat Yronwode made this statement in 1986. "All our books are copyrighted to the creator - they own all the rights.[17]"

> *Miracleman* was originally created and developed as the character "*Marvelman*" by writer Alan Moore (who wrote all of the original scripts and stories) and by comic artists Garry Leach and Alan Davis (with each originally holding a joint one-third property interest). Leach and Davis later assigned 10% of their interest to their business partner, Dez Skinn. Leach succeeded to Davis' interest. When the property was brought to the United States for publication, and due to objection by Marvel

Comics to the "*Marvelman*" name, the character's name was changed to *Miracleman*. Leach and Skinn (then holding a two-thirds joint interest in the character) entered into a publishing contract with a California comic book publisher called Eclipse Comics ("Eclipse"). While aspects of the publishing agreement use "sale" language, the agreement appeared to convey to Eclipse only, on a personal license basis, Leach's and Skinn's license for publication and license rights of *Miracleman* in the United States (other than to the "*Warpsmith Story*," "*Big Ben*," "*The Guys*," and related characters), as the agreement was expressly subject to the caveat that Eclipse had no right to convey rights to any third party other than back to Leach and Skinn. In any event, Moore conveyed no rights, and retained his one-third property interest in *Miracleman* (incorrectly set forth as 30%), and his 100% interest in the scripts and stories. Moore agreed to write new scripts for *Miracleman* publications, with Moore continuing to retain his sole and exclusive ownership of the copyrights to his prior and new work.

Moore wrote comic book scripts for *Miracleman* publications after the agreement with Eclipse through Eclipse-published *Miracleman* comic book issue #16. Moore received copyright ownership attribution of his stories in each issue. Moore then assigned his one-third interest to writer Neil Gaiman and comic artist Mark Buckingham and the Gaiman/Buckingham team took over creating new *Miracleman* comic art stories. Gaiman wrote eight scripts for *Miracleman* comic books published prior to 1995 under a written agreement with Eclipse, under which Gaiman retained the sole and exclusive copyright ownership of Gaiman's scripts and stories, and also received a portion of Eclipse's interim interest. Buckingham created the comic art for those stories and retained the sole and exclusive copyright ownership of Buckingham's art for those stories. The copyrights to the art for the other scripts were similarly retained by the artists who created each issues comic art.[18]

The contract between Eclipse and Quality Communications, who published *Warrior*, as signed in 1985 clearly shows that the *Miracleman* trademark was not transferred. The transfer of ownership rights was also clearly set out.

"Eclipse shall not assign or otherwise dispose of its rights in the ownership hereunder to any third party except to Rights Holder, or a new corporation or entity in which the majority stockholders of Eclipse are and remain the majority stockholders or managing partners.[19]"

In simple terms, this meant that Eclipse could not sell *Miracleman*, or the stories, to anyone, even under Chapter 7. Once Eclipse went bankrupt, the rights and ownership should have reverted back to the original owners, as outlined in the Agreement between Eclipse Enterprises and Quality Communications, which were Dez Skinn, Garry Leach, Alan Davis, Alan Moore and Mick Anglo.

What McFarlane did buy was a dead trademark for the logo to *Miracleman*, the stylized 'MM' that appeared on *Miracleman's* costume (registered July 14, 1987). This was not the name, nor was it the character. The 'MM' logo was as unique to *Miracleman* was the 'S' shield is to *Superman*. The character is separate, you can still have *Superman* stories without the 'S' shield, in the same way that *Miracleman* could still exist without the 'MM'. After all, the name had been changed at least once before, from *Marvelman* to *Miracleman*.

McFarlane also bought the trademarks to Eclipse Comics and *Airboy*. Those three marks were the only ones owned by Eclipse.

Why did McFarlane believe he owned *Miracleman*?

One of the documents handed to McFarlane after the sale was a letter from the Eclipse lawyer, Robert Donnelly. In this letter, addressed to Dean Mullaney, Donnelly makes mention of registering three trademarks, one of which is listed as *Miracleman* (the other two are Eclipse Comics and *Airboy*), however, what was registered was 'MM'. This is the only document in the sale that mentions the character, by name, other than a list of books and film that was being handed over. McFarlane did not look beyond this letter to the accompanying registration certificate, which clearly shows the 'MM' logo and not the name *Miracleman* had been registered. The law firm handling the bankruptcy sale also advised McFarlane, via Terry Fitzgerald, to do their due diligence with regards to the trademarks bought. It is not known if that happened. As it stands, a simple search of the US Trademark Office would have told McFarlane that he was not in possession of *Miracleman*. Such knowledge would have saved a lot of people a lot of angst.

Also muddying the waters was the statement issued by the Trustees with regards to the rejected Marlow & Company offer, which stated, "Copyrights, trademarks, characters and other intellectual property, film negatives and color separations, related to and comprising the *Miracleman* comic book series and publishing agreements with any authors, illustrators and other rights holders in connection with the *Miracleman* comic book series". The only publishing agreement that has come to light was the contract to write the series signed by Neil Gaiman. The Trustee had been guided by Eclipse as to what was owned in regards to *Miracleman,* if they had done their own dull diligence then it is entirely possible that they would have discovered that Eclipse did not own copyrights to the early material, as published in *Warrior*, nor did they own any trademarks, other than the stylized 'MM' logo.

McFarlane later said in his deposition that he ordered TMP to get rid of the comic books and trading cards, but, naturally, to keep the art, film, color separations and negatives.

Handbags at Dawn: Rob v Todd

> "I have only one thing to say at this time: Whatever court this goes to, it will be fairer than the kangaroo court they've been conducting." – Rob Liefeld

> "If you want me to describe Rob Liefeld right now: Rob as in Rob, Lie as in Lie, and then Feld." – Todd McFarlane

Image had been founded largely through the efforts of Rob Liefeld and Todd McFarlane. Both men had a mutual distrust for Marvel Comics, they'd collaborated and communicated and when Liefeld decided to branch out and form a new company, the first person he phoned was McFarlane who went all in. McFarlane was a True Believer in Image and there for the long run, unfortunately it appeared that Liefeld wasn't.

The first publisher of Image was Tony Lobito. His title was in name only, he was only able to act with the full approval of the six Image partners, Liefeld, McFarlane, Jim Lee, Marc Silvestri, Erik Larson and Jim Valentino. For Lobito this proved be an almost impossible task. As Image grew, each man went off into their own studios and began to pursue their own agendas, so getting all six to agree on anything became a rarity.

Enter Larry 'Beanworld' Marder. Marder came from a solid background of advertising and comic books. He was asked in his 2002 deposition to detail how he came to work in the comic book industry, starting with his first job in 1973. "I was in the advertising business. I was an art director in the advertising business and worked my way up to vice-president and creative director of the Sandra Allen Advertising in Chicago, Illinois. (From there) I was publishing my own comic book called Tales of the Bean World. Tales of the Bean World was self-published and it was distributed by Eclipse in 1985. 'You pay for the comic and we'll distribute it.' And I would do some marketing work for them and in exchange for that they would publish -- they would distribute my comic. In 1991 I went to Moon Dogs, a chain of comic book stores in Chicago, and I was the marketing director. I left Moon Dogs because my contract was up and I didn't know what I was going to do next and then I received a phone call from Image asking me to come out and talk to them."

Marder's role was to replace Lobito and become the Executive Director of Image Comics. The role wasn't going to be an easy one. "My duties were to oversee their collective business of their partnership, to oversee the office. There were six shareholders, Jim Lee, Todd McFarlane, Rob Liefeld, Eric Larsen, Marc Silvestri, Jim Valentino.[1]

"The guys felt that they needed to restructure the Image office and they were looking for someone a little older and more experienced than the crew they had together. They called me, and I agreed to come out to the offices for a two- or three-week period where I was going to write a report and help them assemble a short list of people who could help them oversee the Image office. That was two and a half years ago. I never wrote the report, and there never was a short list. From the first day I walked in the door, everybody started treating me as though I was in charge. There were two stacks of paper on my desk that first day, each about a foot-and-a –half tall, of all the problems that needed to be solved, so I started solving them. Unfortunately, though, it seems as though they never all go away.[2]"

"My concern was that they wouldn't let Larry do what they wanted him to do," Valentino told *The Comics Journal*. "But very much from the get-go they treated him as a peer. Larry was used to the Six Marx Brothers Routine that the partners carried on. His job was to be a small voice of reason. This would be a guy who would come in and tell you 'No,' someone to be a sounding board, an advisor, a mediator. They had to respect his decision-making process. His actual job was to direct the executives, to keep misunderstandings down. He's a consigliore, a diplomat. And he takes information in his head and turns it into coherent press releases. Todd described Larry's function as being to protect the 'i,' and he did it very well for us for six years.[3]"

No matter how good Marder was at his job, cracks began to appear in the Image façade as early as 1994. Liefeld had formed another company, Maximum Press, and was publishing comic books outside of the Image imprint. Those inside Image began to believe that Liefeld, who was, at the time, Image's chief executive officer, chief financial officer and secretary, was pursuing his own agenda, to the detriment of Image itself. Accusations began to fly of financial misappropriation, poaching artists from other Image partners, using Image staff for work done on behalf of Maximum Press and Liefeld's suspected plans to move titles out of the Image imprint and into Maximum Press.

This was too much for Silvestri who moved his own studio, Top Cow, out of Image in June 1996. "When Marc Silvestri chose to leave in protest that he felt he had been substantially hurt by an Image partner," Marder later said, "it was the first time I realized Rob was no longer willing to reach a compromise to hold the partnership together.[4]"

"I needed a change," Silvestri said. "Top Cow[5] had been developing a pretty good name for itself, and we'd done a few things that people had taken notice of and appreciated. I felt that I needed to take what I had built and see what I could do with it on its own.[6]"

In 1996, Lee and Liefeld returned to Marvel to draw and write the company's *Heroes Reborn* storyline, featuring a relaunch of the *Fantastic Four*, *Avengers* and *Captain America* titles. This caused further problems with the Image partners, with McFarlane becoming the most vocal in public.

"I don't care how these guys want to spin doctor it. It's always amusing to me. First Rob and Jim went and did the Marvel '*Heroes Reborn*' thing, and they were all 'Well, we grew up with these characters, and we love them and...' And it's always a bunch of crap. The reason they went and made a deal with Marvel Comics was that they got a ton of cash. End of the conversation. Finito. Rob Liefeld did what he did, God bless him. And Jim Lee did what he did, God bless him. But they're the competition now.[7]"

When launching the *Avengers* title, Liefeld had asked Valentino to write the book. Valentino subsequently handed in his first storyline to praise from Liefeld. Then Liefeld changed his mind, Valentino wasn't going to write after all, instead Liefeld wanted him to merely script the book[8]. Valentino deiced to leave and went public claiming that Liefeld had not paid him for his work. "This is to inform everyone that as of this morning I have resigned from The Avengers due to non-payment," Valentino wrote on an on-line message board. "I want to make it clear that Marvel is blameless in this unfortunate turn of events and that I am looking into suing Rob Liefeld for monies owed and wrongful termination. Obviously, more will follow[9]."

More followed... "Let everyone know what a low-down dirty rat bastard Liefeld is to do this to someone who has been so supportive of him over the years. And let everyone know that a day of reckoning is at hand and Mr. L is about to reap the whirlwind.[10]"

Liefeld was quick to respond. "Jim Valentino said, 'I haven't been paid.' You know what? We coughed up every check, and Jim Valentino went away. That was bullshit. It's like, 'Nice try - liar, liar. Here's all the check stubs, you were paid up until Avengers # 4, Avengers #1 hasn't even shipped yet, and you're telling people.' I mean, nice attempt to slander me.[11]"

The camel's back finally broke in September when press releases were issued by both Image and Liefeld. Liefeld's release announced that he was resigning from Image, Image's release clearly stated that he was being punted from the company he'd helped form.

Liefeld wrote to the Image partners. "It has become apparent to me by your recent actions that it is your intent to not only drive me from the company I helped to found, but also to destroy my career in the process. These actions have had a severe emotional impact on my wife and me. In light of these circumstances, I have no choice but to resign as a member of the Board of Directors, Chief Executive Officer, Chief Financial Officer and Secretary of Image Comics, Inc.[12]"

The Image partners, which included Silvestri, had unanimously voted to show Liefeld the door a mere thirty minutes before his resignation letter was received.

"There's legal ramifications as far as what we can say about it," Silvestri said. "All I can say is that pretty much, he earned the vote... it's not something that ever came up before, with any member. We've never even come close to saying [any] person should be out of the company in the years that Image has been in existence... it's just safe to say that severe things have been happening."[13]

"I'm not sure why it was necessary for them to take the action they took," Liefeld said. "And I'm confused why there was so much hostility towards my resignation. I made my decision, I'll live with my decision. They're welcome to say whatever they want, but I have nothing more to say, other than that I really enjoyed working with them and had a good time. I think we had a really cool company together.[14]"

In response to the claims that had been made against him, both privately and publicly, Liefeld decided to go one step further and, on October 5, he filed suit against McFarlane, Lee, Silvestri, Larsen, Valentino and Image Comics for slander. He sought $7,600,000 in damages for the slander and libel, along with an additional $200,000 he claimed was still outstanding from the sales of Liefeld produced Image comics.

Liefeld's complaint alleged the Image partners were guilty of wrongful termination for the manner in which they removed him, and breach of contract for money that he claimed Image was withholding from the sales of his comics.

There were fifteen counts against Image and the partners.

1) Breach of Contract

2) Breach of Fiduciary Duties

3) An Accounting and Valuation of Image Comics, Inc.

4) Conversion

S) Breach of Implied Covenant of Good Faith and Fair Dealing

6) Constructive Trust

7) Equitable Relief, Including an Injunction and Specific Performance

8) Common Count for Money Had and Received

9) Libel and Libel Per Se

10) Slander and Sunder Per Se

11) Gross Mismanagement

12) Waste of Corporate Assets

13) Abuse of Control

14) Interference with Contract and

15) Wrongful Termination

In his complaint, Liefeld argued that there was no difference, legally, between Image Comics and Lee, Larsen, McFarlane, Silvestri and Valentino. As far as the complaint was concerned, the five men were Image Comics.

The Image partners fired back with a cross-complaint which finally revealed the extent of the allegations from their camp. Not only was he owed nothing, Liefeld, according to the cross-complaint, actually owed the Image partners the balance of a million-dollar overpayment in addition to almost $250,000 that he had misappropriated from the Image head office to pay expenses for his own Extreme Studios and Maximum Press imprint.

The cross-complaint also alleged Liefeld had stolen creative assets from the company and coerced Image employees into doing unpaid work for Extreme Studios. Other allegations included a damning one that Liefeld had copied pre-publication artwork from other Image artists for use in his books and had used the Image name and reputation as leverage to force vendors to provide services to Maximum Press on credit. Finally, it was alleged that Liefeld had violated California business laws by using Image resources and knowledge to set up a competing business to Image Comics in the form of Maximum Press.

Image called for damages in excess of $1,200,000 which included $85,000 in funds overpaid to Liefeld and more than $240,000 for money that Liefeld had allegedly used to pay his own expenses. The cross-complaint claimed Image had suffered financial losses and damage to its reputation as a result of titles that had been marketed and solicited through Image but taken out of Image's hands when Liefeld departed to start his own line.

It quickly became a public slinging match, with both Liefeld and McFarlane leading the way for their respective sides.

"I called up and said, 'Hey, I'm going to resign'," Liefeld said. "I called Jim Lee.

'Jim, I understand there's hostilities. Rather than prolong this out, I'm just going to resign.' 'Okay. That probably is a good thing.' Erik Larsen: I got choked up with Erik. Erik's an old pal. Erik was like, 'Yeah, I understand. I'm sorry this happened.' Valentino, call him, he's fine. I don't talk to Silvestri, didn't need to. At the time, he wasn't on the board[15]. I tell Larry Marder, 'You know, look, I'm going to resign so we don't have to have a big fight.' Word comes back: 'Todd doesn't care. He doesn't care that you're resigning. He still wants to vote you out. He wants to kick you out.'[16]"

McFarlane was vicious and brutal in his rebuttals. "Rob basically hasn't paid some of his bills and has lied to people and has told them false stories and intimidates people. Those aren't lies given that you have people who basically have told you. So again, all the people we ended up talking to, the few that we did, we didn't have to do anything because he ended up pissing on all of them anyway. So it all came to pass anyway...we just said: 'Rob, you owe us some money. So now that you're out of the company, don't go away mad, just go away. But this money you took from us that none of us were aware of, could we please just have it back?' And his response to that was: 'I'm going to sue you.' To some extent he should never have taken the money in the first place. He just crossed a line. But if he had just paid it back then that would have been okay. But to find out we got outstanding bills for *Avengelyne* shit, then it's like, that's problematic. So essentially we just got so fed up with it that to me it was like: 'Let's just kick him out and let him sue us because he's going to do it anyway.'[17]"

It didn't take long before a clue into the real reasons behind McFarlane's anger was revealed. "I've heard what he says about me and they're fucking lies. Like that I owe him money. That when I did my *Youngblood* toy, I owe him money for my *Youngblood* toy. Which is a crock of shit and I got the fucking checks to show it. Go talk to those kids and you see how much money they've got out of those checks I've given Rob Liefeld. You'll see that the answer probably is zero, because Rob Liefeld is probably telling them some fucking lie again. Which I know he is to some of them, that he's never gotten a penny from me. 'Ah, good. I'll give you the money when I get it from Todd. But Todd's never paid me because Todd's a crook.'[18]"

Cooler heads quickly intervened, and it was here that Marder showed why Valentino hired him in the first place. Marder began to mediate the dispute after being approached by Jim Lee. Lee was clear, settle the suits, quickly, quietly and away of the courts where everyone's dirty laundry would be aired.

Larsen, Valentino and Silvestri all agreed with this strategy. However, McFarlane was keen to get Liefeld on the stand and was insistent that Liefeld would not get a cent from Image. No matter how hard Marder tried, McFarlane wouldn't budge, so Lee placed a call to McFarlane who finally gave his consent.

"The whole thing was just so unnecessary," Marder said. "These types of litigations take up a tremendous amount of time, energy and resources, and it's rarely worth it. But he litigated against us first, and we had to protect ourselves. We collected on everything that he owed us and we ended up exactly where we started [monetarily].[19]"

"You have to understand, there was never a time when Marc and Rob were gone," Erik Larson later reflected. "It was Marc left because of Rob, and then as soon as Rob was out of the picture he came back. It was fun. In order for Rob to get kicked out, it did have to be something to be voted on by all of the partners, and Marc was still a partner and had to be there. So it was 'Hey - we know you! You're our pal! C'mon!' But no, it really was a matter of simply choosing. You know, Rob and I don't really hang out terribly much these days. Rob just got kind of bent out... I don't really pull any punches. I just kind of say 'Oh, gee that's shit,' if I think it's shit. And apparently, there were a couple of times when I said things that hurt Rob's feelings so it's his own view at this point.[20]"

"I think he's the last guy on the planet to know that nobody cares about him anymore," McFarlane told *Wizard*. "He talks, but there's nobody listening. It's unbelievable how he can make the glass half-full when it's half-empty 'I'm stronger for going to war against Marvel and Image.' Every one of his defeats he can make sound good. 'I needed to downsize.' No, everybody quit because you weren't paying them! The one that amused me the most was where he said, 'I couldn't wait to get out of Image.' For six months, and I'll show you the fucking bill, for six months he and his lawyers prevented us from trying to get him out of the company. For six months they blocked it, every time we tried to get him out he blocked it, and I just read where he said, 'I couldn't wait to get out; I wanted to do nothing but leave.' Yeah? Well, then, why did we both get $50,000 bills saying the exact opposite?[21]"

The handbags at dawn had done irreparable damage to Image Comics and the relationships of the six men who'd founded it. The dream was now over. The partners would reunite, eventually, but that would take over a decade and things would never be the same.

Eventually Jim Lee would leave Image to work at DC, taking with him all of his creator owned properties, which he sold to DC. Larsen and Silvestri would work at both Marvel and DC. Valentino would become publisher of Image Comics in 1999 and remain in that role until 2003.

Tony Twist Sues

Once back on writing duties, McFarlane continued with the story of *Spawn*, including more encounters with Antonio Twistelli. As one dimensional as the character was, Twistelli continued to pop up. He appeared in a number of *Spawn* comics and became somewhat popular with McFarlane's readers. All was good with the world, that is until the real-life Tony Twist saw an issue of *Spawn* and saw the name of the mobster described as being a 'fat pig'.

Wizard Magazine, then edited by McFarlane's friend Gareb Shamus, didn't help matters. Each issue the magazine featured what it called a 'casting call'. This segment was designed to pair up comic book characters with actors who'd be perfect casting for films. When it came to *Spawn, Wizard* were very clear who should play the mobster, Tony Twist. "The Mafia don that has made life exceedingly rough for Al Simmons and his loved ones, in addition to putting out an ill-advised contract on the Violator, is named for former Quebec Nordiques hockey player Tony Twist, now a renowned enforcer (i.e. "Goon") for the St. Louis Blues of the National Hockey League.[1]"

What Twist saw angered him. According to court filings, he became aware of the existence of *Spawn* and of the comic book's use of his name for that of the villainous character. On one occasion, several young hockey fans approached Twist's mother with *Spawn* trading cards depicting the Mafia character *Tony Twist*. Subsequently, at an autograph session Twist was asked to sign a copy of the *Wizard* article in which McFarlane was interviewed and Twist's hockey trading card was pictured.

The mystery is why did McFarlane named his character Tony Twist? It wasn't that McFarlane hid the fact that he named his characters after hockey players. In a reply to a letter, published in *Spawn* #20, McFarlane openly admitted to this, and included Twist's name as an example. McFarlane was again asked about his naming conventions for a *Wizard* special and replied that Antonio Twistelli was indeed named after Tony Twist, with *Wizard* doubling down and describing him as a "...former Quebec Nordiques hockey player, now a renowned enforcer (i.e., 'goon') for the St. Louis Blues of the National Hockey League.[2]"

McFarlane was evasive, but had to admit, under oath, that he was aware of the real Tony Twist when he named his character. "As I sit here today, I don't really know how it came up at the beginning. At some point somebody said, "Hey, Todd, you know, it's the name of a hockey player," and it was, like, cool, Tony Twist, cool, it's a hockey player. I looked him up, went, "Cool, he's right, cool," and that was it, yeah.

"That's what I'm saying, whatever the answer is, sir, it wasn't a big enough deal for me to give him a name in Issue 6, so again, could I come up with Tony Twist? Yeah. Was it Antonio Twistelli? At some point though, yes, there's a character named Tony Twist and, yes, I know that there's a man sitting there named Tony Twist. So, yeah, all that, I'll admit to all of that, yes, yes, yes.[3]"

To others, he told different stories. According to McFarlane, he told Rob Liefeld that none other than Stan Lee had given him some advice along the lines of naming characters with the same initials or first and last names. Lee's examples of this include Peter Parker, Matt Murdock, Pepper Pots, Happy Hogan, Stephen Strange, Reed Richards, Wyatt Wingfoot, Sam Sawyer, John Jameson, Robbie Robertson, Betty Brant and, of course, the ultimate, the tri-initialed J Jonah Jameson. There are, obviously, more.

The concept of naming comic book characters with the same initials for first and last names wasn't originated with Stan Lee. This practice goes back to some of the earliest characters in the medium. The granddaddy of them all, *Superman*, had Lois Lane in his first appearance, back in *Action Comics* #1 in June 1938. Over the ensuring years Lex Luthor, Lucy Lane, Lori Lemaris and many more followed. This wasn't limited to comic books; there were cartoon characters such as Porky

Pig, Bugs Bunny, Mickey Mouse, Donald Duck and Betty Boop. The list is almost endless.

As an aside, this is not to say that Stan Lee told McFarlane that he originated the practice. And if he did, that claim is easily debunked. Lee, having worked in the industry for nearly two decades when the Marvel Universe, as we know it, was originated, would have been very familiar with the idea of naming characters. It's highly likely that Lee was just passing on an easy, and some would say lazy, way to get character names.

Another of McFarlane's excuses was that he was familiar with Brooklyn gangster Abe Reles, aka 'Kid Twist'. Surgically adept with an icepick, Reles was a hit man for Murder Inc. in the 1920s and '30s and gained his nickname of 'Kid Twist' from any one of three sources. 'Kid Twist' had previously been the nickname of Max Zwerbach, an even more obscure Brooklyn gangster who died in 1908, two years after Reles was born. It could have been Reles favorite candy, or it might have been given to him due to his penchant for throttling people with his hands (that is when he wasn't stabbing them with his icepick through the ear). In any case, Reles was the more famous of the two 'Kid Twists' and McFarlane later claimed he was familiar with him. Where this theory fails is that it's a long stretch of the imagination to get to the name 'Tony' from either Max, Abe or even 'Kid'.

But the Reles story explains the 'Twist' side of the name, the Stan Lee story, when combined, explains Tony. Tony Twist. But, as can be seen, McFarlane changed his story, depending on where he was and who the audience was at the time. To his fans, it was clear, and McFarlane had admitted it, Antonio Twistelli was named after hockey player, Anthony Twist.

It's hard to know what McFarlane's true motives were, but it can be theorized that he believed the players would be flattered and amused to now become comic book characters. Whatever the real reason, McFarlane kept on with his characters names, and Twistelli even appeared in the Alan Moore written *Violator* mini-series and was a character in the HBO animated television series. Tony Twist, a supporting character, was there to stay. But Tony Twist, the hockey player, wasn't flattered, or amused. In fact, he was angry.

An angry Twist wasn't to be taken lightly. Throughout his hockey career, Twist had built a reputation of being a 'goon', the type of player who is picked less for their playing abilities and more for their skills in fighting. Twist had a long career beating players up on the ice.

> "Left-winger Tony Twist has been a part time grinder and enforcer since entering the league in 1989-90. He was tough battler in the corners as well as a reliable checker.[4]"

Twist took exception to the HBO series as well, claiming that it showed the fictional Tony Twist "wearing pink G-string underwear and talking on the phone while two naked women, who are not his wife, engage in sexual behavior beside him; arranging the murder of a news journalist; as a member of the Mafia; smoking cigarettes; using abusive and profane language; sleeping in bed with two naked women, who are not his wife, who are then murdered; hiring hit men and assassins to conduct multiple murders on his behalf; arranging to have a child kidnapped; expressing frustration and anger that the kidnapped child has escaped; and, dangled high over a city as retribution for all the evil he has perpetuated". According to Twist, both the comic book, and now the HBO series, had portrayed the fictional Twist, and thus his name, in several unflattering, and potentially career damaging ways, including, "a "Mafia" crime boss; a solicitor of prostitutes; an abuser of women; an abuser of alcohol and cigarettes; as a murderer; a sexual deviant; a kidnapper of children and as greedy, uncharitable, uncaring, cowardly, insane and having other undesirable traits".

Twist did what most Americans do when faced with such a situation – he sued. In 1995 Twist alleged that McFarlane had been using his name, along with his image and likeness, without permission or authority. McFarlane would be able to argue the latter two claims, but the first claim would be difficult. Twist then went on to allege that McFarlane was experiencing a financial gain from Twists name, while he (Twist), was experiencing losses along with serious damage to his name and reputation.

McFarlane, who believed he was insured against such a claim, promptly sent the claims to his insurance company. The insurance company, Hanover Insurance, looked at both the complaint and McFarlane's policies and began to hedge their bets, openly stating that the claims for coverage did not fit the criteria for which McFarlane was insured for.

Hanover Insurance's stance came from several loopholes. The first was that two of McFarlane's companies, and there were several, Todd McFarlane Productions and TMP International, were named in the complaint along with McFarlane himself, were un-insured, unlike McFarlane.

Another loophole for the insurance companies came with the time line. McFarlane introduced the Twistelli character into *Spawn* in 1992. This was prior to Hanover's involvement with McFarlane, which didn't come until May 1995 to May 1998. This meant that Hanover would not take responsibility for any damages from the sales of the offending issues of *Spawn* prior to May 1, 1995. Hanover Insurance made this clear from the start, that they would only be covering part of the total costs. Other insurance companies that McFarlane had bought insurance from in the intervening years, from Citizens Insurance Company Of America, The Travelers Indemnity Company Of America and General Star Indemnity Company, all sought to minimize their responsibilities for the same reasons as Hanover – that the period Twist was claiming relief for did not fall under the timelines for their policies. However, for the time being, Hanover remained tentative with their support, often paying the legal bills put before them.

McFarlane decided not to settle and threw it to the courts, opening a can of worms that would surround McFarlane for the better part of the next decade and a half, cost him millions of dollars and see him lose some of the cornerstone characters of the *Spawn* universe, along with IP that he'd purchased along the way. It would also cost Image Comics money as well, as they were brought into the suits with both Twist and Gaiman and shared the overall costs – in the case of the Twist trial, Image Comics agreed to shoulder 50% of the costs of defending the case.

The longer the cases went on, the messier they got. McFarlane was fighting in various courts, including bankruptcy courts. What also accrued were the legal fees, and, in losing his cases, McFarlane, his insurers and Image, saw those costs increasing by the month.

Of interest is that Twist also sued *Wizard Magazine* and its owner/publisher, Gareb Shamus. Not wanting to get caught up in all, Shamus had his lawyers negotiate a suitable out of court settlement. As the trial went on, HBO did the same.

Another co-accused, TCI Cablevision, who produced the *Spawn Animated Series,* defended on the grounds that it did not base the fictional villain on Twist, that it received no financial benefit, and that its actions were protected by the First

Amendment. Ultimately the jury would throw out Twist's claims against McFarlane's fellow defendants, TCI Cablevision, Titan Books, Grupo Editorial, Blockbuster Entertainment, Hollywood Entertainment, Video Update, and Legends, Comics Cards finding that they were mere 'passive distributors' of the comic books and related items and thus not liable for any damages. This would mean McFarlane would be shouldering the judgement on his own.

The trial began on 19 June 2000. Each side hit the mark; McFarlane argued that the largest endorsement Twist had ever gotten in his career was $20,000. The Tony Twist in the *Spawn* comic bore no resemblance to the real Tony Twist. "In my entire career, I've never said 'based on' ever," McFarlane told the court. "Until I got sued, I didn't know what the word persona meant." Pressed further, McFarlane admitted that the only character that was of any importance to him was *Spawn*. "You could take away 299 characters and leave me with one, *Spawn*," he told the court, adding, with confidence, "I'm in business tomorrow." He then told the court that if he had set out to deliberately base a character like Twist on someone real, he'd have called him Wayneatelli Gretzkytello, adding, "And I would have cut that down to Wayne Gretzky."

Twist's side argued that he would have lost endorsements due to the 'intensely negative portrayal' of the *Spawn* Tony Twist. The losses allegedly incurred by Twist included a $100,000 endorsement from Experimental and Applied Sciences Inc, a performance nutrition and dietary supplement company. This deal was withdrawn, according Sean Phillips, the Vice President of the company, solely because of the use of the Twist's name in *Spawn*. "It would have been lucrative for me," Twist told the court. "And who knows who's turned me down without even contacting me? How can I realistically, say, endorse children's products when I'm involved with this kind of crap? How can they take me seriously?" Twist also argued that McFarlane's habit of hosting *Spawn* nights at minor league hockey games was hurting his earning potential. Twist took the stand and talked about his anguish of having to find out about the *Spawn* Twist via his mother and how the 'vulgar, violent mobster' reduced his earning opportunities. "I felt that the negative impact on me was going to be substantial," he told the court. "My unwilling participation in this infuriated me."

Publicly McFarlane was confident of a win, privately it was different. "My stomach is right about 98 percent of the time and I've got a bad feeling," he told journalist Bill McClellan. "I don't think I'm going to walk out of here clean.[5]"

McFarlane lost the first trial against Twist. The outcome was potentially devastating for McFarlane. The trial court dismissed the defamation count, but sustained Twist's 'misappropriation of name' claim and ordered McFarlane to pay him $24,500,000 in damages, not including costs. Outside the court, Twist repeated the claim about learning about the comic book via his mother.

"My mom said, 'Son, I can't believe you lent your name to this guy.' I had no idea what she was talking about. So I checked it out. In one part of the HBO show, I'm in pink thong underwear, smoking a cigar, ordering the kidnapping of a child while two women are naked on the couch making love to each other. I obviously don't want any part of that. Even if I was a good guy in the comic I wouldn't have participated. You've got kids being kidnapped, you've got nudity, you've got police raping women. It's nothing I want to be affiliated with.[6]"

Twists comments reveal the basic issue with the case – Twist clearly felt that the character was not only named after him, but also *based* upon him. As far as Tony Twist was concerned, he was Antonio Twistelli and anything that Twistelli did reflected poorly upon him as a person. None of the journalists covering the trial thought to ask Twist just what his reputation was. He was an enforcer, a person known to fight others during a hockey game, concentrating on the blows more than the game itself. He may have lost an endorsement, but it's hard to see what kind of an endorsement can be offered to a 'goon' that would appeal to young children.

As if to reinforce Twist's status as a 'enforcer', the bulk of the newspapers showed only two types of photo when reporting on the trial – one was a headshot of Twist, grinning, and usually placed next to an image of the *Spawn* Twist, which showed that the two looked nothing alike. The second type of photo, and the most popular, usually showed Twist bashing an opponent in the head. This continued from the first trial through to the last.

"It's exactly like what I did on the ice - a war, a battle," Twist said. "It hasn't been a drain on me. If it's an emotional drain to go to battle, don't do it, because you're probably not cut out for the job.[7]"

The loss came as no surprise to McFarlane "I would have voted against myself," he told the *St Louis Post Dispatch*, who'd been covering the trial, "And I like me! I thought that 'law' was sort of short for 'logic. That just got blown out of the water.[8]"

'It's not over," he told the *Edmonton Journal*. "I'm willing to go the whole nine yards on this one. I'm taking this very personally. I resent the state of Missouri for taking away my constitutional rights. I'm just glad this part is over so I can get back to work. I can approve more toys this week, read more scripts. This ruling does not affect any of our daily activities. If I'd lost and the damages were only $10 I'd still fight this thing, because you can't let what happen stand. I'm not trying to cover my backside on this. What I was just found guilty of; there are now thousands of people in the entertainment and publishing industry guilty of the same crime.[9]"

It's worth discovering how the jury came up with an award of $24,000,000, plus costs. The jury came to the figure as it represented slightly less than 20% of McFarlane's combined gross earnings, including comic books, toys, books, the animated series and feature film, since the publication of the first issue of *Spawn*. If true, this meant that the jury firmly believed that McFarlane had grossed over $120,000,000 in the ten years from 1992 to 2002.

"I wish I could be impervious to it," McFarlane admitted. "The case we have going is up at the appellate court right now... Hurt feelings [are] not a crime. They were not able to bring one iota of evidence -- other than that someone had hurt feelings -- that a crime had occurred. The question I get is, why did you get a $24 million suit against you? We were at the lowest level of the courts. You'd be surprised at how emotions play into it when you've got a jury that you pick off the streets that aren't lawyers. I don't even blame them. They're laymen, they're not lawyers. They're not listening for the key words, where the judges and the lawyers are listening for the key words. When they say these key words, [the lawyers] say, "Uh-oh, that's a good one" or "Uh-oh, that's a bad one." Whereas these laymen say, "They made his momma cry" or "They made him kick his dog." And then this guy says, "Well, if I don't even own my own name, what do I own?" Well, you do own your name... It's just that you're not the only one with the same. There may be a 1,000 people with the same name as you. In the case of coming up with character names, it's sort of an ongoing thing in literature; various names sometimes cross paths with real people's names. But it's not that person. It's taken a lot of time and money to get to this point, but we're in the driver's seat now. The jury felt sympathetic, but the judge threw everything out. Said it was a farce. Now it's up at the federal appellate courts and argue it all over again potentially.[10]"

With that in mind, it comes as no surprise as to how McFarlane was able to drop

$3,000,000 on a baseball knocked out of the park by Mark McGwire so easily, along with other home run baseballs and Madonna outfits.

As an aside, the reasons for McFarlane buying the baseballs wasn't just due to a love of the game, he had business in mind. "The McGwire ball bought me some meetings. People tend to equate money with success: Hey, that guy spent $3 million for a baseball! Bring him in! It's like buying into a poker table. But then it's what you do once you're at the table. Anyway, I could have spent the money on a couple of Super Bowl commercials, but you think anybody would still be asking about them years later?[11]"

Larry Marder believed it was McFarlane's purchasing of baseballs that became a catalyst for Neil Gaiman to sue. "In 1999 Neil said that he was angry because of Todd's purchase of the Mark McGwire baseball and that none of this has been resolved (between Gaiman and McFarlane). I believe that I told him, you know, that at this point this was not my business and that there was nothing I could do.[12]"

McFarlane appealed decision of the jury, but he would have other cases to occupy his time before it was due to be heard.

Todd Runs Neil Around

Michael David Thomas: The rights to *Miracleman* seem to be a source of controversy that pops up now and again. It's coming back to the forefront. What kind of rights do you have to the *Miracleman* character?

Todd McFarlane: Ultimately? I've got all of them. We'll find that one out.

MDT: You own the rights to the character, lock, stock and barrel?

TM: Until someone proves otherwise.

MDT: The only reason I ask is that Neil Gaiman has cited as a partial owner. But as far as you're concerned, you've got all of that?

TM: Someone may very well prove that wrong, but I'm willing to prove the point. If somebody else thinks that they have control of this, then do something about it. Because I'll be right there on you, right now. Then we will solve this problem.

MDT: Is it something where it's been so murky, you want to get into a courtroom and get it over with, if someone really wants to litigate it?

TM: Nobody wants to litigate anything. It's a matter of people moving on with life, making a call as to what's a priority. If somebody feels as strong about *Miracleman* as I do, then I invite them to take as hard a stance as I will. If somebody steps that way, then we'll let somebody else decide which of us is right. Maybe neither of us will be. Maybe we'll both partially will be. Who knows? Until any of that happens, then I take the position that I own *Miracleman*.

MDT: Have you heard from Neil Gaiman or his representatives?

TM: Yeah.

MDT: And have they said anything in particular about threatening litigation?

TM: Let's just say that we don't see eye-to-eye[1].

While he was fighting with Twist, McFarlane was negotiating with Neil Gaiman over monies owed and promises broken.

Angela, the character that Gaiman had created and introduced in *Spawn* #9, had proven to be somewhat of a hit with the readers. It didn't hurt that Gaiman was writing the character, but, other than the one-off payment of the not inconsiderable sum of $100,000, Gaiman had seen very little out of the character. McFarlane was producing *Angela* action figures and reprinting Gaiman written stories while seemingly fobbing Gaiman off with promises of payments.

In 1995, Gaiman decided to take the lead and began to address these issues with McFarlane.

"Todd did a *Medieval Spawn* toy. It was one of his first rollouts of the toys. He credited me, unasked, which I thought was very nice of him as the co-creator of the character on a comic that came out with the toy and later sent me a check for $20,000, which although it didn't come with any breakdown of how it was derived, and in fact, I think just came with a helpful note "This is from Todd because we love you," or something like that, I was told on the phone was my royalty share of the *Medieval Spawn* toy, which I thought was really cool.

"So I have been paid money for the toy, don't know how it's been arrived at, but it's $20,000 and that seems a fair amount to me and Todd seems to be living up to his hey, you can trust me and I'm looking after you side of the deal. Then 1995, late 1994, early 1995, the *Angela* toys are out. I remember being incredibly proud when they made the cover of USA Today as the most inappropriate toy of the year, according to the American Family Association. And I would hear from Todd that they were selling incredibly well and that they were incredibly popular, cool, the Angela toys.

"And I thought great; I will get a royalty on these. Nothing ever happened, no payment ever came in. I would ring Todd's people and say "Is there a payment," and they would go "Oh, yeah, yeah, don't worry about it, we are not businessmen here." Todd would say that a lot, that he wasn't a businessman, he was a creator and you just had to bear with a certain amount of disorganization and his funny way of doing things. So I waited. Never saw any royalty. I had written the Angela miniseries. And the main reason I had actually written the *Angela* miniseries was my son, Mike, at that point was 13, going on 14, if memory serves, and he had found a copy of Spawn or he had found one of these Medieval Spawn toys and said this is really cool.

"And he started asking me, you know, 'Dad, why didn't you write something I could read. I love this *Spawn* stuff.' So I found Todd and said 'Okay, I think I'm – it looks like I'm going to be writing another series for you. Let's do *Angela*. And let's do it as a three-issue miniseries.' And Todd said great.

"Anyway, *Angela* comes out. I hear from them. Todd didn't like trade paperbacks. Todd had said to me several times just in conversation there were things he didn't like and he didn't like trade paperbacks because they weren't proper comics and he didn't trust them. Meanwhile, I was making a huge part of my income from trade paperbacks and saw that there was an enormous demand for them. So at one point in there they said we are going to be bringing out *Angela* in trade paperback. And I said great, we should work out a royalty deal on this. I was feeling less comfortable by that point with the idea, so I said to them do we have a royalty deal on this? Up until that point the only the way that things seemed to work was one would get these checks and they would say here is a check for $800 because Todd thinks you are a good guy. And I actually saw in the press at one-point an. Interview with Todd where he was saying no, we don't do royalties, we just send people love checks and they are better than any royalties could ever be. So I didn't trust the love checks and I went out to

Phoenix. I talked to Todd. I do remember talking to him. I have no recollection of what the substance of the conversations were in '95.

"Toward the end of '95 about I think I was getting a little bit testy here, I felt like there were no checks coming in, he had these things and he was not paying and there seemed to be no real effort to pay. And I was concerned that, as I said earlier, that Todd could either sell the toy business to Mattel or he could get hit by a truck and there would be no paper records of any kind of deal and I thought we needed to memorialize it.[2]"

McFarlane saw another way to appease Gaiman. It was a move that he felt would cost him far less than what he now owed. He would give Gaiman *Miracleman*.

"I was hoping that there may be a wild card in the deck called *Miracleman* that may or may not have some value, and so if we sort of hit some snag where we couldn't resolve some of the issues that maybe there is a sort of a more non-traditional way to resolve it by going let's do a character swap or a hostage swapping, if you will, you know, of some of the characters. And so *Miracleman* potentially became that.[3]"

The meeting in Phoenix didn't go as well as planned, with neither side seemingly capable of being able to see the other's point of view.

Neil Gaiman was quite clear as to what he saw happen at the meeting.

"Todd kept saying 'but you can trust me and I will send you, I will send you bigger checks than you will get if you have a contract.' And I said 'Todd, call me silly, but I would much rather have a written contract and $500 in royalties than $1,500 that is going to turn up on a whim and could end the moment that you decide it's not convenient.'

"He said that he thought that was crazy and I said that that was how, you know, just assume that was how I was billed. And we then wound up – then everything ended very badly in terms of Todd had to wrap up rather quickly. Larry Marder had come out for that meeting because they just learned that Marc Silvestri had left the Image partnership that day, so they had to sort of get on the phone and try to sort that out.

"The way it was left, ended was Todd saying 'Do you trust me?' I said 'I trust you completely.' He said "Good. Then I will work this out in a way that is going to be fine." He said "I'm really pleased you came down here. You have been completely reasonable and we will sort this out." And he also said that, he mentioned to me he just bought *Miracleman*. And he said 'What are you going to do with *Miracleman*? What are you thinking about?'

"I said 'I don't know at this point.' And he said 'Well, I have had lawyers look over the agreement that you made with Alan Moore and we think we could break it, but obviously we are going to honor it. So you have -- you know, we are going to respect your third of *Miracleman*, but we need to figure out what it is and it may be a bargaining chip." And I said "Well, that's fine.'[4]"

In a last-ditch effort to bring things back on track, Larry Marder was brought in to help mediate a settlement between the two creators. At the time, Marder was working for Image Comics in the role of Executive Director.

"I was asked by Todd or Neil if I could help mediate whatever misunderstandings there may have been at that point in time. I called Neil and said, that's my understanding that I should try to -- try to bring everybody to some sort of terms and that I was willing to give it a try. I asked Neil what he thought it should be, I believe. We were talking about Angela, Medieval Spawn and Cagliostro. We were trying to establish the terms of Neil's DC contract because Neil said that -- that we were trying -- what we were trying to do is attempt to define what rights he may have had under his DC contract, because I believe we were trying to match his DC contract.

"Neil sent me a fax saying that he believed that this is the way that it broke down. I wrote it up in a sheet for him to try to figure out if what he was telling me over the phone and what he had written down, to put it in a more logical fashion. I submitted it to Neil and we talked about it on the phone and I made some corrections. And then I think I asked if I could see the relevant parts of those contracts or if I could actually see the contract and he sent me some materials, but they were red lined and they didn't seem like the final version to me, but I submitted it anyway.

"I submitted it to Todd to show him that this is what we believe from my discussions with Neil, that this is that these are the terms of his DC contract. I think what happened was Todd kept it for a while and then -- and then I worked out the work-sheet for Todd that would have some sort of counter-proposal or some sort of understanding as to ways of defining these things with questions regarding some of -- some of the language because the language, I think it was imprecise.

"My goal was to get them to come to some sort of agreement that both sides could agree upon. Neil would say that he was looking for something comparable to his DC agreement. Todd was saying, 'I don't understand what these terms mean.' So Todd dictated a counter-proposal.

"I spoke to Neil. He asked me some questions. I don't remember. He asked me some questions, and then I spoke to Todd and we clarified what Neil asked. Then from my point, I don't believe I talked to Neil again after that until we received a letter from Neil's counsel rejecting the whole thing.[5]"

The deal being offered to Gaiman was, in his eyes, far worse than his DC Comics contract for *Sandman*, so he had no problems in rejecting it. The two parties met again, this time in Oakland, to discuss the problem. They began the process of thrashing out a deal, and in June 1997, McFarlane phoned with an offer of a swap - *Cogliostro* and *Medieval Spawn* (subject to McFarlane accounting for and paying Gaiman current to date) for McFarlane's giving to Gaiman all of McFarlane's claims, involvement and tangible property in respect of *Miracleman*. Gaiman agreed.

> This is to confirm the main points touched on in our conversation of July 15, 1997. You agree that with regard to the character of Angela, her appearances, spin-offs, merchandising and foreign translations of Spawn 9 or the Angela mini-series, that you'll be using the figures we put together based on the DC deal (I'll attach my letter to you following the Oakland meeting to this).
>
> That my rights in *Cogliostro* and *Medieval Spawn* as above will be exchanged for your share of *Miracleman*. However, you will make all payments up until the date of exchange for the use of the characters, based on the same figures as above. You'll include whatever you have in the way of inventory or film for *Miracleman*, received from Eclipse in the bankruptcy buy-out.
>
> The date of exchange will be that of the first accounting, currently planned for August 1st.
>
> That there will be a $5,000 'bonus' paid to me on the handover fee,

essentially as an apology for having dragged this thing on so long.

That I have, exclusive of any other *Angela* projects I might do with the Todd McFarlane division of Image, the rights to do a one-off *Angela* comics project, and a one-off *Medieval Spawn* project, on each of which I would keep 100% of the revenue: that if these are team-up projects they could go to other comics companies, but if they exclusively feature the character in the title, I agree to do them with Image (although not necessarily with you). That you will make your best efforts to ensure that there is a "created by Neil & Todd" credit for *Angela* in her appearances in other comics, or other media.[6]"

The clauses pertaining to *Angela* were important for Gaiman, as he'd already broached the possibility of *Batman/Angela* and *Phoenix/Angela* crossovers with DC Comics and Marvel respectively. As Gaiman would author them, both companies were very receptive.

"I started talking to DC Comics and to Marvel Comics," Gaiman told the court. "To DC Comics I talked to a man named Denny O'Neil, who was the editor of *Batman*, about doing a *Batman/Medieval Spawn* book and talked to Mike Carlin, who was the editor of the *Justice League* titles, about doing an *Angela* crossover at DC and talked to a man called Chris Claremont, who was an editor at Marvel about doing an *Angela/X-Men*. Getting a feeling for what we could do.[7]"

It was here that alarm bells started sounding for Gaiman. It appeared that nobody could reach McFarlane to discuss the projects.

ARNTSEN: Did you talk with anyone in Todd's companies about these one-off projects?

GAIMAN: Yes. I spoke to Larry Marder and later to Beau Smith.

ARNTSEN: First, tell the jury about your conversation with Larry Marder.

GAIMAN: I told Larry that I was looking to do these things and couldn't put a deal in place unless Todd could confirm with the companies that we had this deal as written in the thing.

ARNTSEN: What did Larry tell you?

GAIMAN: He'd talk to Todd about it. Todd was really busy.

ARNTSEN: And Beau, who's Beau Smith?

GAIMAN: Beau Smith was somebody who'd originally worked with Eclipse. He later went on to work for Todd on the toy front. And Beau was working in some capacity and I'd known him for years. I phoned him and said, "I really want to get these projects under way. Can we get something out of Todd in writing so that we can just move on with it?"

ARNTSEN: And what did Beau Smith tell you?

GAIMAN: He said, "Sounds good to me. I'll talk to the Toddmeister.[8]"

August 1 came and went without the exchange happening. McFarlane sent over the physical materials that he'd bought from Eclipse, related to *Miracleman*, but not the trademarks or the rights to the character. Nor any monies or accountings. Instead of giving Gaiman *Miracleman,* McFarlane began the process of registering the trademark for the character.

At this stage, Gaiman threw his hands in the air. He decided that McFarlane was never going to honor his various promises, so he handed the situation over to his lawyer. It would take another four years for the case to come to court.

The reason for the final breakdown between the two men has always been in dispute. Gaiman maintained that McFarlane never honored the agreement that the two had worked out. McFarlane felt that Gaiman kept changing the overall parameters of the deal to the point where it became impossible to honor. All through the dispute he had been taking advice from Terri Cunningham, who was in charge of contracts at DC Comics. Cunningham had been telling McFarlane how the royalty system operated and deeper negotiations went with Gaiman, the more McFarlane relied on what he was being told. Eventually Gaiman asked for one thing too much.

"I went over the ongoing conversations we had, what we had talked about potentially confirming in Oakland and put all that again feeling that Medieval Spawn who was sort of the big crux in my sort of ongoing conversations, was that I essentially all of this from my perspective was just to get Spawn back and that, and that whatever I had traded, I felt that I was trading for something I already had. So at this point I was I'm going to keep all of this.

"And one of the things we had talked about is maybe continuing to give ongoing accounting on *Angela*, but even that, I mean, we are essentially down to *Miracleman* and potentially Angela. That's all we have got at this point. He's got my money. He's got my money. I'm not going to get money back out of this guy. Let's just cut this thing completely now.

"But to get near the finish line made me feel pretty good and given this is August, the *Spawn* movie's coming out, I'm trying to enjoy life. To find out that some of the information that had been a constant source of discussion may not have been completely forthright was becoming wearisome to me, and so again at some point the straw broke the camel's back. Neil in good faith had been receiving moneys trying to get the calculations that we were giving him based on what we thought was truthful information and he had my money and my character and was giving me back something that essentially something that we had that he had represented that he had which from my perspective he didn't and I was never going to get money back from Neil. I didn't think that would ever be true. So I had to grab something. The only thing that was still left was I gave him money and *Miracleman*. The money was gone and so I told him to get *Miracleman* back.

"Neil in trying to settle it gave me some more numbers that when I had another follow-up conversation with Terri she told me that those numbers were not correct either. So now we're in a spot where I don't know where the beginning of truth is on what it is because we are essentially almost back to square one of going 'what are we talking about now' because we can't seem to get a handle or at least from my perspective I can't get a handle on what it is that we're even trying to resolve because now we're going, 'Well, who has what?'

"It may have been on how you spend money on people in movies or television shows or on how they divide those moneys up. I don't recall the specific numbers. I just felt that whatever it was again was inconsistent with information I was getting. I think it may have been I think it may have been film, Hollywood stuff maybe.

"It might have been actually just a general breakdown of that category. I think most of the numbers that that Neil and I passed back and forth to each other were representatives. I don't remember the specifics. All I remember was that at the end of the conversation going, 'another inconsistency,' and that was my emotional break at that point.

"So I called Terri Cunningham. I don't remember the specifics other than I got the same answer which is, 'No, it wouldn't work that way, Todd.'

"This is the proverbial straw on the camel's back. So this is why that conversation isn't as nearly important as to the ongoing burden leading up to this. So that clarifies it hopefully.

"From my point of view, then everything up to that point was rescinded and null and void. I'm done. I'm done. I'm done. He's got money. I have been giving him money at this point based on things that may or may not be true. He's been feeding me potentially things that are not completely truthful. He potentially has taken as a swap a part of this, *Miracleman*. And so I get suckered. I got suckered here and I just went, 'No, no. It's not going to happen.'

"I may have gotten on the phone and went, 'You know what, grab *Miracleman* back because that wasn't a fair swap.' After that, between Neil and I, dead silence. Later on I think after he wasn't getting payments he was going, 'What's happening? What's happening? Where's my payment?' I think I sent him out a letter sort of stating that there was no deal.[9]"

In a classic case of Rashomon, Gaiman saw things differently. "The specifics of ownership interest were never discussed. I would never have pushed for a 50-50 ownership of *Medieval Spawn* because I felt it was a derivative character. On that, although yes, I was the creator of the character, I would not have felt that I was owed a 50 percent share in him. In the case of *Cogliostro*, absolutely.

"I got a response from Larry Marder after a while that came back with a fairly pitiful offer. And I thought this is very strange and very silly. I phoned Larry and said 'Well, can you explain some of this stuff to me? Can you explain how net is going to be calculated,' and so on and so forth. And he said 'No, I cannot. You will have to trust Todd.'

"Then he sent me another version of that with a little more information about the toys on it, and I looked at these and I thought well, these are not what has been promised and this is not -- this isn't even I thought we were working together. The last thing Todd said is 'You can trust me,' and I'm going I can trust you and so on, so forth. And now he is coming back with this is the deal and it was, you know, these two percent of net for this and half a percent of net for this. I'm going what, that's not what we are into. This is, you know, ridiculous.

"I was under the impression that everything was fine. Even as late as I think March, April 1989 we got a healthy royalty payment through, from foreign stuff, from Mr. McFarlane's wife, actually very nice, came straight from Wanda, a check for about $4,000. And I thought great. I didn't think anything of it at that point, there was anything problematic. And then in the summer I remember talking to the people from DC and from Marvel Comics and saying great, I'm going to do these comics, do these one shots, are you interested, do you want to do them.

"I think I was looking at trying to decide between doing an *Angela/Justice League of America* and an *Angela/X-Men* at Marvel and probably doing a *Medieval Spawn/Batman*, because I had an idea for something that would work for that. I mentioned it to these people and then I would ring them up later and say what's happening and they would say Todd is just not calling us back; we wouldn't be put through to him, which I thought was a bit odd.

"Then toward the end of 1998 there had been no payments of any kind on anything coming in and that was about the same time that I sent the fax to Mr. McFarlane saying by the way, can I have a photocopy of whatever you got, and didn't get anything from him and then went on tour. I was on a signing tour for my book *Stardust*. And I got to San Francisco, I think it was, on the tour and got a message from my assistant that a Fed Ex had just come in from the mail drop. We have a Minneapolis address and a home address. And it had come in from there, from Todd McFarlane. And I said great, well, when I get home, I will have to look at it.

"I was on this 30-city signing tour, so everything was waiting till it was done. And then I got home and I looked at this thing from Todd and it was completely bizarre. It was a letter saying I rescind my previous offer. I'm going what previous offer, we had a deal, and we said we would exchange on the 31st, we did, you paid, and that was our deal. And then it said and now my new deal that I'm offering you is this, and my new deal is I keep, I take Angela back, I give you back *Miracleman*. I said you gave me *Miracleman*, what are you saying here, you are taking back one thing in exchange for one thing that I held onto.

"Then he said if we don't have this agreement, then I'm taking *Medieval Spawn* royalties out of all future royalty. I'm going but you already subtracted 20,000 that you paid me for the toy out of what you paid me for the last thing, you know. We were looking at $1,000 or whatever, I have to see the exact figures, and the total of *Medieval Spawn* toy payment is $6,000. He said I have to recoup that and whether he stuck with that or not, I don't know. He may be carefully counting down his recoup, but I rather doubt it. At that point it was into February 1999. I'm off tour. I'm exhausted. So I got back and I was wiped. And I read through the stuff from Todd and I sent it off to my lawyer at that point.[10]"

Even though an agreement wasn't reached, McFarlane was impressed enough by Larry Marder's efforts and promptly poached him from Image Comics, tapping him to be President of TMP International and to run the toy division. This would prove to be no easy task as the toy division had grown very rapidly and was now a bit of a mess.

"When I came over from Image Comics, one of the first things that Todd said to me was, you already know how to do comics, I want you to learn the toy business. So I spent two years working over the garage with Todd in the headquarters. So I had no responsibilities with comic books. I felt that we needed to streamline the organization in the various departments, and to create managers of each department as a way to make the operations much more efficient, so each manager would have specific responsibility.[11]"

As negotiations broke down, the final word went to Gaiman. At the end of the final meeting Gaiman stood up to leave and McFarlane, angered, spoke. "I'm going to bury you, it's going to cost you $250,000 in legal fees to fight me."

Gaiman looked at McFarlane. "Well," he calmly said, "I'm just going to have to write another $250,000 screenplay on the plane ride home."

Gaiman didn't write a screenplay on the plane ride home though. Instead he contacted Joe Quesada at Marvel Comics.

Since becoming the Editor-In-Chief at Marvel Comics in 2000, Quesada had made no secret of his desire to have Gaiman writing for Marvel. Each time Quesada had touched base, Gaiman would say no as he hadn't written an on-going comic book series since the end of *Sandman* at DC in 1996. However, now he had a plan.

He accepted the offer and formed a company, Marvels & Miracles LLC. Marvels & Miracles would exist to serve only one purpose, to regain *Miracleman* from McFarlane. A press conference was assembled, and it was announced that all of the proceeds to the, as then untitled, series would be handed over to Marvels &

Miracles for the express purpose of funding the legal battle with McFarlane. It wasn't quite the $250,000 screenplay, but, in effect, Marvel Comics would be funding the legal battle between Gaiman and McFarlane.

In the meantime, McFarlane made moves to bring *Miracleman* back to print, announcing that the character would be appearing in *Hellspawn* #13. A cover was drawn by Ash Wood and the comic solicited, only for McFarlane to back out at the last minute after a very public complaint from Gaiman.

The Miracleman Trademark

McFarlane's first attempt to take ownership of *Miracleman* came when he applied for the formal trademark on October 27, 1997. Once he filed the application was assigned the US Serial Number 75,379,919 and all that was required was the proof that the mark, *Miracleman*, was actually in use.

Instead of using the mark, McFarlane sat back and did...nothing. The application was formally abandoned on July 3, 2000. The reason given was, "Abandoned because no Statement of Use or Extension Request timely filed after Notice of Allowance".

McFarlane seemed content to let the application lapse and Gaiman took no action, this time.

As the Gaiman court case loomed, McFarlane must have been told, or realized, that he, in fact, did not own the trademark for *Miracleman*.

His earlier attempt at registering the trademark had lapsed, and *Miracleman* was very vulnerable for anyone to claim it. All that person would need to do is file a trademark application and pay the fees. With a new legal battle looming, McFarlane acted.

On July 1, 2001, he quietly filed a formal trademark application to the trademark in the name of Todd McFarlane Productions. The trademark, #76,283,194 was accompanied by a supporting declaration.

> I, Todd McFarlane, declare that I am properly authorized to execute this application on behalf of the Applicant[1]; that Applicant has a bona fide intention to use the mark shown in the accompanying drawing in commerce on or in connection with the above-identified goods; I believe Applicant is entitled to use the mark in commerce; to the best of my knowledge and belief, no other person, firm, corporation, or association has the right to use the mark in commerce, either in the identical form thereof or in such near resemblance thereto as to be likely, when used on or in connection with the goods or services of such other person, to cause confusion or mistake, or to deceive, although I acknowledge that others claim to have a copyright interest in the MIRACLEMAN character and comic books and I believe I am the owner of any existing copyright in the MIRACLEMAN character and comic books by virtue of an assignment from Eclipse Enterprises, Inc.; that all statements made herein of my own knowledge are true; that all statements made herein on information and belief are believed to be true; and further being warned that willful false statements and the like are punishable by fine or imprisonment, or both, under 18 U.S.C. § 1001, and that such willful false statements and the like may jeopardize the validity of the application or any registration resulting therefrom. Signed this 1st day of July 2001

The declaration shows that McFarlane knew he did not have ownership of the trademark and that Gaiman would be challenging him for it. The wording also shows the ambiguity between Todd McFarlane and Todd McFarlane Productions.

Another issue was that Eclipse had never assigned the trademark to McFarlane. They had never owned it and could not assign or transfer what was never theirs. Sadly, this claim would never be fully challenged in court.

His application was immediately challenged, but not by Gaiman. A manufacturer of swimwear, A & H Sportswear Co., Inc, did take action. They had registered the Miracleman name as part of their swimwear line and duly filed an opposition to McFarlane's application. McFarlane failed to reply, so the application was suspended. In order for McFarlane to have used to name during that initial registration period, he would have to had fought A&H.

Once Gaiman discovered what McFarlane was doing he lodged his own objection under the guise of Marvels & Miracles.

Gaiman listed eight grounds of opposition to the *Miracleman* trademark.

1. Opposer[2] is the owner by assignment of all right, title and interest in the mark, including such assets associated with the mark as films of graphics and publications depicting the MIRACLEMAN character, as well as collateral rights in the mark, including, but not limited, to the right to use that mark on clothing, toys, motion pictures, pre-recorded videos and other media.

2. Opposer has adopted and has continuously used the mark in connection with the comic book character, MIRACLEMAN, and on publications, through its predecessor-in-interest, Neil Gaiman, since at least as early as 1990. Moreover, the public recognizes Opposer as related to its predecessor-in-interest, Neil Gaiman, who is Opposer's Managing Director.

3. Opposer will be injured and damaged in its continuing use of the mark in connection with the character, MIRACLEMAN, and on publications featuring that character and bearing the mark by the registration by Applicant of the mark, MIRACLEMAN for "Printed matter, namely, comic books and posters," "Clothing, namely, shirts, athletic shirts, T-shirts, caps and jackets," and "Toys, namely, action figures and accessories therefore."

4. Application Serial No. 76-283,194 for registration of the trademark, MIRACLEMAN, for "Printed matter, namely, comic books and posters," "Clothing, namely, shirts, athletic shirts, T-shirts, caps and jackets," and "Toys, namely, action figures and accessories therefore" was filed by Applicant on July 11, 2001 and was published in the Official Gazette of November 13, 2001.

5. Through its valid and continuous use of the MIRACLEMAN trademark in connection with publications, and the character, MIRACLEMAN, featured in those publications, the trade and purchasing public have come to associate the mark with Opposer through its predecessor-in-interest, Neil Gaiman, and have come to recognize publications so marked as originating with Opposer.

6. Applicant's mark, MIRACLEMAN, and Opposer's mark, MIRACLEMAN, are

identical and the goods sold by Opposer and the goods intended to be sold by Applicant under the MIRACLEMAN mark, as set forth in the application, Serial #761283194, herein opposed, both include publications, including comic books.

7. The MIRACLEMAN trademark of Applicant, as intended to be used on the goods of Applicant set forth in its application, so resembles in appearance and commercial impression the trademark, MIRACLEMAN, as used by Opposer, that as applied to the goods of Opposer, it is likely to cause confusion or cause mistake, or to deceive.

8. Based on the foregoing, the registration of the mark depicted in Application Serial No. 75-283,194, filed July 11, 2001, on the Principal Register of the United States Patent and Trademark Office will cause injury and damage to Opposer in its ownership and use of its trademark, MIRACLEMAN.

The trademark application was then placed on hold pending the outcome of the civil case.

"I think he thought, 'Gaiman's a pussy'," Gaiman told The Comics Journal. "The nice thing about being a best-selling author is that, while I can't afford to buy a hockey team, I can afford a legal case. Getting involved in filing a lawsuit was not high on my list of things to do, but I'm perfectly willing to see where it all will go. Under no circumstances would I be willing for him to use the (*Miracleman*) character. Let us begin with his behavior over the character so far: announcing he was going to publish *Miracleman* without even coming to me first. There are complete graphic novels that I wrote for Todd McFarlane Productions in print all over the world without me being paid a dime. Even Marvel at its worst would never have done this. Why would anyone go back after all that?[3]"

Faced with the suspension of the case, A&H pressed forward and were handed the trademark for *Miracleman* (#4459354). Their trademark covered the use of the name for clothing, in particular swimwear. This now meant that anyone else could file for *Miracleman* for comic books and other media, but not for swimwear. As A&H had no desire to publish comics, their only stipulation would be that no clothing appear with the name upon it.

The trademark case, which, as mentioned was wholly dependent upon the outcome of the Gaiman v McFarlane case for *Angela*, *Medieval Spawn* and the other characters created for *Spawn*, would never be tried. It would remain in limbo until McFarlane abandoned the application and effectively handed the character over to Gaiman, who would, in turn, hand it to Marvel Comics.

First Gaiman Trial

> "I said, what would happen next was that a jury of Americans would decide whether to trust an Englishman or a Canadian.[1]" - Neil Gaiman.

In the end, the jury, consisting of six married women and one unmarried female college student, believed the Englishman. The make-up of the jury would become a reason, for some, as to the verdict.

That court battle in 2002 ended with a win for Gaiman and a crushing blow to the reputation of Todd McFarlane as a fighter for creator's rights.

On the stand McFarlane was brutalized with many inconsistencies in statements, both present and past, being revealed.

> ARNTSEN: Now take the *Angela's Hunt* trade paperback. That was published by Image in 2000, correct? You never told Neil you were publishing that book, did you?
>
> MCFARLANE: I don't recall.
>
> ARNTSEN: That book has Neil's biography on the back of it, doesn't it? Or a synopsis of it?

MCFARLANE: Yeah, a write-up.

ARNTSEN: It doesn't list any other creator other than Neil Gaiman? Greg Capullo's not listed on the back, is he?

MCFARLANE: No, sir.

ARNTSEN: And you've never paid Neil anything for *Angela's Hunt*, have you?

MCFARLANE: If you say so.

ARNTSEN: And you'd agree with me, sir, that if somebody uses a creator's name without their permission, they're dishonoring that person's reputation, correct?

MCFARLANE: What's the question again?

ARNTSEN: You would agree with me that when somebody uses a creator's name without their permission, they are dishonoring that person's reputation?

MR. FELDMAN: Objection. Calls for a legal conclusion.

THE COURT: Overruled.

MCFARLANE: Yeah, I wouldn't necessarily say that.

ARNTSEN: Here. There's a letter column in *Spawn* 7, correct?

MCFARIANE: Right.

ARNTSEN: That was a common practice you had in at least your early issues of *Spawn*. You'd answer letters from readers, correct?

MCFARLANE: Right.

ARNTSEN: And do you recall saying in an answer to a letter in *Spawn* 7, "In order to advertise an appearance by a particular person, the store owner needs the consent of that person."

MCFARLANE: OK.

ARNTSEN: Do you believe that sir?

MCFARLANE: OK.

ARNTSEN: And then further down you say, "When somebody uses a creator's name without their permission they are dishonoring that person's reputation."

MCFARLANE: OK.

ARNTSEN: Do you dispute that you said that, sir?

MCFARLANE: No, sir.

ARNTSEN: This would also apply co using a person to advertise a book, right?

MCFARLANE: You know what? I haven't read that, so I got to see in what context I said that. So you're - I don't know what the question was, and you're asking me another - can I, can I read it and see what he was asking me specifically?

ARNTSEN: Sure.

MCFARLANE: OK, now I've read it. This is - is there a question there?

ARNTSEN: Sir, did I correctly read your statement in your answer to that letter?

MCFARLANE: Right[2].

The key factors of the case were presented to the jury as follows: Gaiman was asked, not hired, to write *Spawn* #9. His work on the title was not done under a work-for-hire contract. In the process of writing the script for *Sawn* #9, Gaiman created two new original characters, *Angela* and *Cogliostro* along with a derivative character named *Medieval Spawn*. Gaiman also wrote a partial script for *Spawn* #26, along with a three issue *Angela* mini-series, which had been collected and reprinted as a trade paperback.

Spawn #9 had sold in excess of 900,000 copies.

Between the years 1992-1996, Gaiman received $194,983 in payments for his contributions to the *Spawn* and *Angela* comic books and related products.

In or around April 1997, Gaiman and McFarlane met to discuss the terms of the compensation that was then due. On May 5, 1997 correspondence between the parties detailed the percentages due Gaiman. On July 15, 1997, Gaiman and McFarlane discussed the same matter by telephone. Gaiman sent, via fax, written confirmation of the discussion, and his understanding of the agreement reached during that discussion. On that same day McFarlane faxed back his assent with request for clarification on certain points. Gaiman responded by fax to clarify the points raised by McFarlane on the same day. The agreement reached as of July 15, 1997 provided, in part, that Gaiman would have the right to do additional literary projects with the characters *Angela* and *Medieval Spawn*, which may involve other characters from different publishers. Gaiman's rights to *Cogliostro* and *Medieval Spawn* would be exchanged for McFarlane's rights to *Miracleman* and that exchange would be effective as of the date of accounting for amounts due. July 31, 1997 was agreed to be the date of accounting and exchange or if necessary when the final accounting was completed. TMP started to produce some of the accounting information by August 4, 1997 but, as of 2002, the final accounting was still not complete.

During the accounting process in 1997, Gaiman received a payment of $22,407, which included $5,000 unrelated to the unpaid royalties. This brought the total royalty payments received by Gaiman for his contributions to the *Spawn* and *Angela* comic books and related products to $212,390.

As payments had stopped in 1997, royalties were due for *Angela, Red Angela, Medieval Spawn* and *Cogliostro* toys, *Spawn-Angela*, *Angela* and *Prey for the Hunter* posters, *Spawn* trading cards and POG sets, *Spawn* TPB #2 and #6, *Curse of the Spawn* issues 9, 10 and 11, foreign printings of *Spawn* #9 and *Angela* along with all other appearances of *Angela*, *Cogliostro* and *Medieval Spawn* in both comic book form and in other media, namely the HBO *Spawn* animated series and the New Line Cinema *Spawn* motion picture.

Gaiman's biography and name had been used, without Gaiman's knowledge or permission, in connection with the publication of *Angela's Hunt* by McFarlane. Similar uses of his name and biography had netted him $45,000, so this was due.

The jury found that Gaiman had a copyright interest in the works at issue, McFarlane had breached Gaiman's right of publicity under Wisconsin law (for which he was due damages and mandatory attorney fees) and that McFarlane had passed off Gaiman's works as his own, in violation of his rights under the Lanham Act.

The full verdict, as recorded by the jury, was as follows:

1. Does plaintiff Neil Gaiman have a copyright interest in the following? Medieval Spawn: Yes. Cogliostro: Yes. Spawn #26: Yes.

2. Would a reasonable person in plaintiff Gaiman's position have discovered prior to January 24, 1999, that the McFarlane defendants were claiming to be sole owners of copyright interests in the following? Medieval Spawn: No. Cogliostro: No. Angela: No. Angela #1, #2, and #3: No.

3. Did the plaintiff and the McFarlane defendants enter into a contract in 1992? Yes

4. Did the McFarlane defendants breach the 1992 contract? Yes

5. Did the plaintiff and the McFarlane defendants enter into a contract in 1997? Yes

6. Did the McFarlane defendants breach the 1997 contract? Yes

12. Was defendants' failure to identify plaintiff Gaiman as a co-author of Spawn #26, Spawn Volume 6, or Pathway to Judgement a false description or representation of the origin of the work? Yes

13. Does plaintiff Gaiman believe that defendants' failure to identify him as a co-author of Spawn #26, Spawn Volume 6, or Pathway to Judgement is likely to damage him? Yes

14. Did plaintiff Gaiman consent in writing to the use of his name and biographical information on Angela's Hunt? No

15. Did plaintiff Gaiman make misrepresentations or omissions of material fact to defendant concerning his DC Comics contract during the negotiations of the 1997 contract? No[3]

The jury ordered McFarlane and Image Comics pay him the amount of $45,000.00 with costs, which was the maximum amount due for the use of his name and biography, and attorney's fees in the amount of $33,639. McFarlane and Gaiman now shared ownership of the characters *Angela, Medieval Spawn* and *Cogliostro,* along with co-ownership of the comic books *Spawn* 9 and 26 and the three issue, *Angela* series and trade paperback. McFarlane also had to provide an accounting for all the works and TMP and Image Comics were denied permission from publishing or distributing *Angela's Hunt* using the name or biographical information of Gaiman for purposes of trade without his written consent.

The accounting was damaging. McFarlane had paid Gaiman a total of $212,390. *Spawn* #9 accounted for the bulk of that amount and had been broken down to a script payment of $10,000, royalties of $80,000 and a bonus of $10,000 which equaled the $100,000 that McFarlane had promised him. Gaiman had also been paid $3,300 for three pages of script for *Spawn* #26. The *Angela* mini-series saw Gaiman earn $73,651, including trade paperback sales of just over $10,000. Foreign sales had seen Gaiman pocket $5,273 and he'd been paid $24,807 for toy sales and posters.

Elsewhere things didn't look too promising. Two sets of *Spawn* POGS had been a bust. Although McFarlane had been advanced $100,000 Canadian for the rights to both sets, bringing his share to $200,000, Gaiman had been paid $675 for the use of *Angela* and a woeful $34 for *Medieval Spawn*. Nobody wanted them then, and they're still not collectible now.

The trading cards fared slightly better for Gaiman. The *Spawn* Trading Card Set, issued by Jim Lee's Wildstorm, saw McFarlane earn $323,341 in royalties. Out of this Gaiman was paid $1,940. The *Spawn* Trading Card Chromium Set, issued by Topps, generated royalties of $61,818, Gaiman's share was $139. The third set that featured *Angela,* the Image Universe Card Set, again issued by Topps, had generated $15,000 for McFarlane, Gaiman saw $61.00.

The amount now due to Gaiman was estimated to be owed an amount as low as $269,255.33 to as high as $300,743.18.

Not that Gaiman was overly thrilled to now be part owner of the *Spawn* universe. As far as he was concerned, that ship had well and truly sailed. "In 1997 going on to 1998, maybe even to 1999, the idea of me doing a *Medieval Spawn/Batman* story, for example, would have had some value. The idea of *Angela* and the *X-Men* would have had some value that *Angela* would have brought to the table.

It's now 2002 and frankly *Spawn* doesn't sell very well anymore. The comic is a not very well selling comic. The characters are not very popular characters. *Medieval Spawn* is long since forgotten. And the kids who had bought the toys are now throwing up in colleges. Even *Angela*, he killed her off as a character in *Spawn* 100. I look at it, and what would be incredibly attractive to any publisher is me doing a book, but me doing a book with *Medieval Spawn* brings no value to the table.[4]"

McFarlane now owed Gaiman an immediate payment of $45,000 in damages, was liable for Gaiman's costs and after the accounting, as much as $300,000 and change. Not only that, but he had lost the copyrights to both characters and issues of *Spawn*. This would cost him money down the track, as any collected editions of *Spawn* would either be missing issues, or he'd have to negotiate with Gaiman, and pay, for their inclusion.

Professionally it was massive blow to McFarlane who had long rallied for creator's rights. By appropriating Gaiman's characters, and not paying him, there were some who pointed out his apparent hypocrisy and noted that, by all appearances, he was no better than the companies he'd often complained about, notably Marvel and DC.

McFarlane instantly appealed to the Seventh Circuit, which noted that the judgment was not final and limited its consideration to the injunction requiring McFarlane to acknowledge Gaiman's co-ownership of the copyright. The Seventh Circuit also dismissed the violation of rights under the Latham Act. It wouldn't be the end of it though, and the case would head back for retrial.

But the case had been about *Angela*, not *Miracleman*, so McFarlane announced plans for a statue, and reactivated his plans to bring the character back in the pages of *Spawn*. This prompted Gaiman to finally act.

"I used to think that McFarlane actually had some rights in *Miracleman,*" Gaiman wrote on his on-line journal." He told me he had, after all -- he'd bought what was left of Eclipse from a bankruptcy court -- and that he very much wanted to swap those rights for my rights in *Cogliostro* and *Medieval Spawn*. He never sent me any of the papers, though, after I agreed to the '97 character swap, although he sent me the film for several issues of *Miracleman*. Then, a month after sending me the film, and having told me that he had transferred his rights in *Miracleman* to me, he sneakily filed an application for the trademark on

Miracleman. Then a year or so later, he abandoned that trademark application. (This was something I didn't know, but that came out in the run-up to the court case.)

"During the legal case, the one thing that no-one was confused about was that I, and Mark Buckingham, and Alan Moore, owned the copyright to our work in *Miracleman*. That was straightforward and obvious. We owned our copyright on our material; the bankruptcy of Eclipse didn't affect our rights. Actually that's not quite true. Todd said in some interview online before that he owned all rights to *Miracleman* and if anyone said different, he'd see them in court. Well, he saw me in court...

"As part of the court case, we finally got to see the *Miracleman* paperwork. It turned out the entire paperwork that Todd hadn't sent me consisted of an expired Eclipse Trademark registration for the MM logo. From another source I also got to see the original contract, under which Eclipse had obtained their license to a part share in the Miracleman character, and it was explicit in saying that in case of Eclipse folding, or even substantially *changing* directors, that Eclipse's share in the rights to *Miracleman* would revert.

"So one thing that the court case did establish was that Todd obviously didn't, as he had been claiming, own all of *Miracleman*. As far as I can tell, or any of the lawyers working with us on the case could tell, Todd probably doesn't actually own any share of *Miracleman*. He certainly has no copyright in any of the existing work. Currently (as of late 2001) Todd has another trademark application in on *Miracleman*, on the grounds that it was an abandoned trademark, which we've opposed. There may well need to be a final court case to tie up some of the last loose ends on *Miracleman*, which may wind up going to some very fun places indeed. At least with 1602, there's the money there to fight it. And there are a lot of places that want to republish the work that's been done on *Miracleman*, and the new work that Mark and I hope to do.[5]"

The trial wasn't without controversy. In the same way that McFarlane felt that the Tony Twist trial had gone against him because the *Spawn* version of Twist allegedly made Twist's mother cry, it was felt, by some, that Gaiman had charmed the all-woman jury. This resulted in misogynistic comments from certain creators who couldn't accept Gaiman's win for what it was.

"Just between you, me and the lamppost I think it had more to do with the all-female jury at the trial," Dave Sim wrote to Erik Larsen. "It wouldn't matter what Todd and Neil were disagreeing about, an all-female jury was going to find Todd in the wrong and Neil in the right just because Todd is Todd and Neil is Neil. Had the judge asked them, I'm sure the all-female jury would have been happy to give Neil the rights to *Spawn*, Todd's house and cars, Madonna's uniform from *A League of Their Own* and the Mark McGwire baseball and anything else Neil expressed an interest in..[6]"

Erik Larsen also took aim at the jury. "It seems patently unfair that Neil could claim ownership of *Spawn* on a horse much less that an all-woman jury, charmed by his English accent and sad story would award him that.[7]"

At the end of 2002, McFarlane was faced with losing two major court cases, and looking down the barrel of $25,000,000 in damages, plus lawyer's costs. And the amounts were rising.

Todd Gets A Win

In the meantime, the Supreme Court of the United States considered McFarlane's appeal in the Tony Twist trial. The appeal centered around a violation of the First Amendment of the Constitution, that being freedom of speech. McFarlane was supported by writers such as Michael Crichton, Larry David, Jeremiah Healy, Elmore Leonard, Harry Shearer, Ron Shelton, Scott Turow, Paul Weitz, and The Authors Guild, all who signed their names to a brief of Amici Curiae.

> *The First Amendment fully protects writers' choices to name characters after famous figures. Authors such as Aldous Huxley, Robert A. Heinlein, Paul Simon, and Steve Martin have all done this, for many reasons: historical or literary allusion, absurdist humor, homage, and more. These are eminently legitimate literary decisions, as other court decisions (with which this decision creates a split) have recognized. So long as the use is clearly fictional, and thus conveys no false statements of fact, it must remain constitutionally protected.*
>
> *The Missouri Supreme Court reasoned otherwise, concluding that in this case "the metaphorical reference to [plaintiff], though a literary device, has very little literary value compared to its commercial value." Pet. App. 19a. But First Amendment law does not allow judges and juries to compare the relative weight of the literary and commercial value of a*

discrete passage or reference in a work. Such a subjective and indeterminate test leaves writers with little guidance about when they may use a particular literary device-which is one reason why First Amendment law generally protects speech, including entertainment, with no regard for a judge's or jury's assessment of its "literary value."

The case was simple for the writers, the Missouri decision violated the rights to free speech by authors, including McFarlane. To illustrate this, famous works were quoted, from Huxley's *Brave New World,* which featured the characters Bernard Marx, Lenina Crowne, and Benito Hoover, which allude to Karl Marx, Vladimir Lenin, Benito Mussolini, and Herbert Hoover, to *Forrest Gump,* Fellini's *Ginger and Fred* (Ginger Rogers and Fred Astaire), Paul Simon's *Mrs. Robinson* (Joe DiMaggio) and even *Yogi Bear* (a combination of Yogi Berra and Art Carney's Ed Norton from The *Honeymooners*).

After considering all the arguments, both for and against, the Appeals Court handed down its verdict on 29 July 2003.

While agreeing that McFarlane had named the character after the real Tony Twist, there was no proof that McFarlane had intended to obtain a commercial advantage out of the name. McFarlane's right to Freedom of Speech was also at question. "The circuit court's judgment notwithstanding the verdict is reversed, the judgment granting a new trial is affirmed, the judgment denying injunctive relief is affirmed, and the case is remanded."

It was a major win for McFarlane as it voided the $24,500,000 that had earlier been awarded to Twist. On the negative side, it also meant another court date with Tony Twist.

By this point Twist was retired from hockey. He had broken his pelvis in a motorcycle accident in 1999 and never fully recovered.

Let's Twist Again

> "This thing is like the Energizer bunny. It keeps going and going and going.[1]"
> – Tony Twist

Two weeks before McFarlane went to court in 2004, again against Twist, after more than six years after tentatively agreeing to provide a defense to McFarlane and eleven days after stating its willingness to attend settlement mediations, Hanover sent a letter to McFarlane that was crushing to McFarlane. "I am writing to clarify the coverage position of Hanover Insurance Company (''Hanover")," the letter began, "concerning the above referenced case and to notify you that, under Hanover's policy, there is no coverage for indemnity or for defense for any of the claims asserted in the current lawsuit against any of the insureds identified in the Hanover insurance policies."

The same letter stated, "...coverage is excluded as to all the insureds under the exclusion for "publication of material whose first publication took place before the beginning of the policy period." It is undisputed that TMP Productions published the first Spawn comic book with the Twist character in 1993, well before the first policy date. Based upon the summary judgment papers prepared by Mr. Kahn and the exhibits therewith, it appears that TMP International first sold toys with a Spawn comic book using Mr. Twist's name or likeness in 1994, well before the first policy date. To the extent Mr. McFarlane is being sued for his acts on behalf of TMP Productions or TMP International, coverage is excluded for those acts based upon the first publication exclusion. Also, to the extent that the defendants are held vicariously liable for each other's acts, the first publication exclusion would apply to exclude coverage.[2]"

In a small consolation, Hanover did agree to continue paying 33% of 50% of the legal costs incurred by TMP, but for no more than a total cost of $140 per hour. This 33% of 50% was McFarlane's half of the costs; the rest of that 50% would be paid by TMP Productions and TMP International. The other 50% would be paid by Image. This would mean that had McFarlane lost to Twist again, he would be personally liable.

The case would once again focus on a few facts, did McFarlane know who Tony Twist was when he named his character and, did McFarlane name Antonio Twistelli after Tony Twist? The other factors in the case would revolve around the damage to Tony Twists reputation. This time Twist's lawyer, the delightfully named Bobby Blitz, went in for the kill, asking questions that he already knew the answer for and trying his hardest to impeach McFarlane by getting him to contradict his earlier testimony.

When asked, directly, if he knew of Twist in 1996, McFarlane had to answer honestly.

> Q: In November of 1996, did you know Tony Twist was a hockey player and did you recognize him as his role in hockey, as being an enforcer?
>
> A: Yes.

Later he testified,

> As I sit here today, I don't really know how it came up at the beginning. At some point somebody said, "Hey, Todd, you know, it's the name of a hockey player," and it was, like, cool, Tony Twist, cool, it's a hockey player. I looked him up, went, "Cool, he's right, cool," and that was it, yeah.

McFarlane then did his best to put Twist into the proper perspective for 1994.

> Your client, again -- no disrespect to Mr. Twist -- at that time, if you look at the stats -- cause I now looked at the stats, I'm actually quite fluent

> in them -- actually had no goals ever. I'm a hockey and sports fan, but I can't say that players and so at that point, I may know all 700 players, and so at that point, I may have come across his name, yeah, but did I consciously know that there was a guy who played in the last place team in Canada, that was for the last place team, that didn't score a goal?
>
> No, I'm not that good. I'm a pretty good sports fan, but I couldn't tell you who the 25th guy is on the St. Louis Cardinals, and I'm a terrific baseball fan.
>
> At that time, Mr. Twist, your client, Mr. Twist, was in the beginning of his career, and he since then has grown a little flourished in his career somewhat and has become recognizable. At that time -- and it's my personal opinion so, again, you know, I don't want to be harsh to Mr. Twist there he was on a last place team in a foreign country that for the most part doesn't speak English and hadn't scored a goal.
>
> That, overall, for a sports fan, aren't the kind of things you look for in the guys you sort of follow.
>
> Again, it's not a slight, but it's just the facts of the stats at that time.

But, during a particularly grueling session on the witness stand, his calm demeanor cracked.

> That's what I'm saying, whatever the answer is, sir, it wasn't a big enough deal for me to give him a name in Issue 6, so again, could I come up with Tony Twist? Yeah. Was it Antonio Twistelli? At some point though, yes, there's a character named Tony Twist and, yes, I know that there's a man sitting there named Tony Twist. So, yeah, all that, I'll admit to all of that, yes, yes, yes[3].

McFarlane again raised the defense of Abe 'Kid Twist' Reles and the conversation with Rob Liefeld regarding the advice Stan Lee had given him, but the damage was done.

The trial in 2004 went the same way as the 2000 trial and resulted in yet another loss for McFarlane. The jury found that McFarlane had infringed on Twist's publicity rights. It wasn't as crushing at the first trial though, this time around the jury awarded Twist $15,000,000 in damages, not including costs. Again,

McFarlane appealed. It was too late; Twist instantly petitioned the court to enforce the payment and issued writs of garnishment and summons. Twist asked for McFarlane to turn over all his property, physical and IP, and the banks to freeze McFarlane's personal accounts pending an outcome from the courts.

Before McFarlane could empty those accounts, the Bank of America handed over $45,541 from his personal account. Wells Fargo did the same, only for more, $50,771.

To the media McFarlane was scathing. "We have a system in America where lawyers represent certain people free of charge and they basically get a bigger commission of what they end up getting. You find that if Donald Trump gets in a fender bender, you find that magically, that guy's neck hurts 10 times worse than if he gets hit by anybody else. You'll find many lawyers that will say to their client, "Now, I want you to be very clear. Did you say Ronald Trump or Donald Trump? I need to know because potentially, we got a better case if it's Donald?"

"Most companies carry insurance so most nuisance lawsuits are based upon shaking down insurance money. When you get down to it, the vast majority of stuff that's clogging the courts - the paperwork, the depositions - is trying to shake people down. It's not even the people, they're trying to shake down the insurance companies for the companies that are there. Because the insurance can settle without the consent of the people who are paying the premiums... A sort of sad state we live in.[4]"

Todd McFarlane Productions Files For Bankruptcy

Faced with the insurance companies refusing to cover him for the full amount of any potential loss, as well as fighting a losing battle with Neil Gaiman, McFarlane placed Todd McFarlane Productions into the relative security of Chapter 11 bankruptcy in December 2004.

Unlike Chapter 7, which Eclipse Comics chose, Chapter 11 was the best, logical choice McFarlane could make. As Chapter 11 is for companies only it wouldn't be seen as a shield for McFarlane to hide behind. Chapter 11 would allow him breathing room and allow him to continue to publish and operate, albeit under the guise of the court. The downside was that by electing to 'go Chapter 11' McFarlane, his insurance companies, Twist, Gaiman and Image Comics would be tied to courts for nearly a decade to come, but that wasn't to be known when the filings took place.

This move was able to be done due to the set-up of the McFarlane companies. In order for a *Spawn* comic to be published, Todd McFarlane Productions would commission the comic. It would then assign the work to the creative team, who would write and draw the comic and hand the work back to Todd McFarlane Productions, who would then pay the creators. Todd McFarlane Productions would publish the comic and then liaise with Image Comics, who would then distribute the final comic book.

In simple terms, Todd McFarlane Productions was the company that employed Todd McFarlane to write and draw. And, as the publisher of the offending comics, it was responsible for the work being published in the first place. The directors of Todd McFarlane Productions were Todd McFarlane and his wife, Wanda. This means that Todd McFarlane, as director of TMP, was in charge of hiring himself to produce comic books. Image was responsible for distributing the comics and McFarlane for writing and drawing them.

It is worth mentioning that at no stage did Todd McFarlane, as an individual, enter into bankruptcy. Only his parent company, Todd McFarlane Productions did. McFarlane, as an individual, was still very solvent and had assets to bolster him along the way.

The Court Cases

There was another very real reason why McFarlane filed for Chapter 11 – Todd McFarlane Productions was hemorrhaging money. In 2006 a disclosure statement was drawn up, with a plan to liquidate the assets of Todd McFarlane Productions. The document gives an amazingly clear insight into what McFarlane was facing.

First and foremost, McFarlane was facing six major court cases that would have a direct impact upon the bankruptcy of Todd McFarlane Productions. These cases and their statuses as of March 2007 were as follows:

Doe v. TCI Cablevision, et al

A claim for violation of right to publicity. This was the first brought by Tony Twist (the 'Doe' in the case), and it included TCI Cablevision, HBO and McFarlane over the *Spawn* animated series. This was also pursuant to the Twist Settlement Agreement detailed below and, as with the next case; Twist was expected to file a notice of satisfaction of judgment.

Tony Twist v. Todd McFarlane and Todd McFarlane Productions, Inc.

Action to enforce foreign judgement of $15,000,000 and costs against McFarlane. This was pursuant to what was known as the Tony Twist Settlement Agreement. Twist was due to file a notice of satisfaction of judgment with respect to an appeal. In simple terms, a notice of satisfaction of judgement is as follows: Once a judgment is paid, whether in instalments or as a lump sum, a judgment creditor (the person who won the case) must acknowledge that the judgment has been paid by filing a Satisfaction of Judgment form with the court clerk. This means Twist was due to tell the court that he had his cash, along with a suitable resolution, and was happy for the case to be, finally, closed.

TMP International, Inc., et al., v. American International Specialty Lines Insurance Co.

A claim for wrongful denial of U.S. District Court, District insurance coverage. The case was pending, but a joint stipulation to stay litigation for 120 days had been approved by the Court in March 2007.

Hanover Insurance Company v. TMP International, Inc., Todd McFarlane Productions, Inc., Todd McFarlane and Tony Twist

This was an action for declaratory judgement regarding coverage for litigation. As with all the open cases, this was pending. Also Pursuant to the Tony Twist Settlement Agreement, Twist was due to file dismissal with prejudice of all claims he filed in this case. In March 2007, McFarlane's camp would file counterclaims against Hanover, Citizens, and General Star Insurance Companies due to the three companies' failure to provide a defense, and thus finances, to McFarlane, over the Twist case.

Neil Gaiman et al. v. Todd McFarlane Productions, Inc. et al

Breach of contract, copyright for ownership, violation of right of publicity, among other claims. McFarlane didn't need this one at all as it would prove to be the most damaging, in terms of reputation. The case was pending subject to litigation. To add insult to injury, Gaiman had indicated that he would be seeking a claim of at least $2,000,000.

Marvels & Miracles, LLC, v Todd McFarlane Productions, Inc.

This was a Notice of Opposition against McFarlane, filed by Gaiman, in the US Patent and Trademark Office. Gaiman was claiming that he was the rightful owner of the *Miracleman* trademark and had opposed McFarlane's registration. Proceedings were suspended in 2006, pending the outcome of the above case. Ultimately, after losing the case, McFarlane would abandon the trademark, effectively handing it over to Gaiman.

There have been at least seven other cases for McFarlane to contend with over the years.

Interleg Int'l V. Todd McFarlane. Copyright infringement. Filed 1994, settled 1995.

Vivid Impact Corp v. TMP Intl Inc. Breach of contract. Filed 1996, settled 1997.

TMP International v. NHL Enterprises Inc. Trademark infringement. Filed and settled 2000.

Kiss Catalog Ltd v. Todd McFarlane Prod. Breach of contract. Filed 2001, settled 2003.

New Line Cinema Corp, et al v. Todd McFarlane Prod. Breach of contract. Filed 2001, settled 2003.

Roth Estate of, et al v. TMP International. Copyright infringement filed by Ed 'Big Daddy' Roth. Filed 2001, settled 2002.

TMP International v. Palisades Marketing. Copyright infringement, this time it was McFarlane on the right side for a change. Filed 2003, settled 2004.

The Corporate McFarlane

> "There was an agreement between Todd McFarlane as the creator of *Spawn* which ruled royalties payable by TMP International, Inc., to Todd McFarlane. Todd McFarlane assigned his royalty rights to Todd McFarlane Productions.[1]" – Alan Inglis.

In 2002 McFarlane attempted to explain the difference between Todd McFarlane the person and Todd McFarlane the businessman.

Q: And did you have those kinds of discussions with Neil?

A: Just clarify. Who are you asking the question to? Are you asking it to Todd McFarlane the head of a toy company, the head of publishing, part owner of Image comic books or the individual? So will you ask your question and ask me which one of those people you just asked the question to?

Q: They are all sitting in front of me, so --

A: But they each have a different agenda during their day, a different task to accomplish during the day. I'm sure you do as a father and a lawyer.

Q: And I guess really what I'm looking for are the specific subjects of disagreement that you tried to work through this in your capacity as head of Todd McFarlane Productions and weren't able to. And I'm not limiting it. I'm just following up on your answer that you gave as the head of Todd McFarlane Productions. If a different hat is appropriate, put it on and tell me you're putting it on.

A: Right. Can I -- can I simplify this even more?

Q: Yes.

A: Can we assume that if I don't say anything it is as the head of Todd McFarlane Productions because 99.9 if not 100 percent of this is as Todd McFarlane Productions.

Q: Okay.

A: So, unless I stipulate something different, if I talk about myself I'm talking about myself as the person running Todd McFarlane Productions[2].

McFarlane had at least twenty different business names that he was operating under. The details of the various companies were presented to the court as follows, and I've added McFarlane's own comments to each company, as relevant, from his 2002 deposition, and, where noted, I've also added in the comments from TMP International's former Treasurer and CFO (1996 – 2001), Allan Inglis, who helped set these companies up.

Todd McFarlane Productions, Inc. Creates, publishes, and licenses books and film entertainment based on characters Todd McFarlane has created. *Spawn* being the major character. Todd and his wife, Wanda, own 50/50.

"Doing publishing, licensing, holding the trademarks, doing free-lance art work. I mean, the whole sort of gamut of creating ideas and stuff.[3]"

"Todd McFarlane Productions was not the publishing company. We would refer to it as a publishing company, but legally it was not. Todd McFarlane Productions wrote the stories and drew the pictures that went into the comics, but the comics were published by another company.[4]"

"There was an agreement between Todd McFarlane as the creator of Spawn which ruled royalties' payable by TMP International, Inc., to Todd McFarlane. Todd McFarlane assigned his royalty rights to Todd McFarlane Productions.[5]"

TMP International, Inc. Toy manufacturer and distributor. Todd McFarlane owns 100%. Initially set up to manufacture toys and clothing apparel based on Todd's characters. They are now licensed to manufacture toys and clothing apparel for others. For example: Ford Motor Company to manufacture and distribute toy vehicles and related apparel; Sony Signatures to manufacture and distribute toy *Kiss* figures and apparel, 20th Century Fox to manufacture and distribute toy *X-Files* figures and apparel.

"Most of it is the manufacturing and selling of action figures. I think we have done like the odd vehicle or, you know, a box or something that's a little off center, but, you know, still plastic goods, if you will, plastic toys.[6]"

McFarlane Toys Spin-off of TMP, wholly owned subsidiary entity used to specifically distribute and sell Todd McFarlane's characters and apparel.

"It's the name on all the toys, McFarlane Toys, not TMP International.[7]"

"McFarlane Toys, Inc. says a spin-off of TMP. In fact, TMP International, Inc. wasn't his toy company. McFarlane Toys is a d/b/a, and McFarlane, Inc. was not an incorporated company.[8]"

McFarlane Toys Collectors Club, Inc. Direct mail marketing sales of toys and apparel.

TMP Asia, Ltd. Distributes and sells toys in Asia, mostly Japan and handles manufacturing arrangements with China. Office located in Hong Kong.

"That helps us have an office in Hong Kong. It helps us with our international sales to our various distributors internationally outside of North America.[9]"

McFarlane Toys Canada, Inc. The worldwide holding company for all sales and distribution of toys apparel In Canada.

"That essentially does the same business as McFarlane Toys. It's just that again there are different rules and regulations when you are distributing products up in Canada, so you need another company to sort of abide by certain tax laws and rules.[10]"

McFarlane Worldwide, Inc. Distributes and sells toys and apparel outside of North America.

"You know what; I don't know (what the company does). I've got a lot of accountants and a lot of lawyers and a lot of tax reasons for doing stuff.[11]"

McFarlane Design Corporation. Design Studio.

Todd McFarlane Entertainment, Inc. Todd McFarlane owns 90%, Terrence Fitzgerald owns 10%. Mr. Fitzgerald is pursuing movie, video, games opportunities.

"That is a company that takes ideas into Hollywood and sees if anybody will bite on any of those.[12]"

The McFarlane Collection. Sports memorabilia collection (Mark McGuire's 70th Homerun baseball, etc.)

The McFarlane Foundation. Charitable Foundation set up for Todd McFarlane.

McFarlane Global Operations, B.V. Distributes and sells toys and apparel in Europe.

McFarlane Europe, B.V. Sales and distribution company set up in Rotterdam for European sales. Tax vehicle to hold retained earnings outside of North America.

"Another channel of being able to distribute our toys into Europe.[13]"

TMP Ventures. Inc. Initially set up to funnel Todd's $3,000,000 investment in NHL Team Edmonton Oilers. However, due to taxes, not used and investment was funneled through McFarlane Toys Canada, Inc.

"In fact, I don't recall if it was even created.[14]"

McFarlane Sports Ventures. Inc. Ford Motor made a special Spawn pickup truck. Todd was going to get into spec Racing SCCA Circuit. Todd lost interest.

"In fact, again, I don't believe it was established as it says. It's a dead deal. I mentioned earlier that a license agreement was discussed with Ford Motor Company and that never came to pass. There were no toy cars made from -- as a result of that – under that agreement.[15]"

TMP Equities, Inc, TMP Toys, Todd Toys, McFarlane Motorsports, TMP

Hockey Association.

It is important to note that not all those companies were actively trading at the time of the bankruptcy, but all had money tied up in them. Certainly, by 2004, those companies had been whittled down to a few, namely TMP International and Todd McFarlane Productions.

Assets & Liabilities 2004

Immediately before he filed for bankruptcy, McFarlane took total ownership of Todd McFarlane Productions. For the duration of the bankruptcy period, he would be 100% liable for all the debt, taking the 50% from his wife Wanda. This was probably done to protect his personal assets and to shield Wanda from any penalties or personal debt that might arise. Wanda was still listed as Vice President and Director, but no longer held any common stock in the company.

In 2004 McFarlane Productions listed its assets at approximately $1,029,438 with $740,000 of that tied up in pre-paid legal expenses. He owed $500,000 in a secured loan, had another $71,819 owed to various creators for work done on *Spawn*, two unsecured debts of $247,688 and $703,688. Then there was the $15,000,000+ to Tony Twist and a potentially unknown, yet estimated at, seven figure amount which would be due if Gaiman won the (then) forthcoming court case (which he did). McFarlane also listed thirty three trademarks as assets, they were: *Spawn, McFarlane's Evil Prophecy, Miracleman, Tremor, Medieval Spawn, Spawn Mobile, Spawn Alley, Violator, Curse of the Spawn, Angela, Overt-kill, Violator Monster Rig* and *The Clown*. Some of these trademarks had been filed more than once, and most were considered to be dead, meaning they were inactive, but those which were live were, *Spawn, McFarlane's Evil Prophecy, Miracleman, Curse of the Spawn* and *Angela*.

McFarlane Production's main creditors were Tony Twist ($15,000,000 plus costs and interest), law firm Riezman Berger ($3,000,000 for legal services rendered to Twist), Solano Holdings and Investments (a $500,000 loan), Neil Gaiman, McFarlane Toys ($683,901 or monies loaned and advanced, and for administrative fees), Brian Haberlin ($13.600), Comicraft ($2,200), Brian Holguin ($8,800 outstanding for writing *Spawn* #144 and #145) and Tom Orzechowski ($2,200), Others listed on his service list included artists Greg Capullo ($18,250), Angel Medina ($3,960), Jay Fotos (5,600), Greg Scott ($1,700) and Danny Miki ($4,070).

In total, McFarlane owed $20,668,827 as of 17 December 2004. And it wasn't going to stop there.

McFarlane was forced to list everyone that he owed money to, including an outstanding check of $60 owed to the Register of Copyrights at the Library of

Congress.

In 2004, Todd McFarlane Productions had posted a net loss of $283,254. This was down on 2003 where he posted a net loss of $423,976. McFarlane Productions total assets, in 2006, were valued at $1,238,722, against total liabilities of $2,594,489.

More people jumped onto the case as time rolled on, notably Film Roman, the company who had developed and produced the *Spawn Animated* series. They claimed $1,208,651 in 2005 for the total costs incurred in making the series.

Among the down valued assets that McFarlane had paid big for were two Mark McGwire baseballs. These baseballs were ones that McGwire hit for his 1st and 69th home run of 1998, which had cost him $219,550 and were now valued at $20,000.

McFarlane still owned the 1998 70th home run ball, which had cost him $3,000,000, along with the outfit that Madonna wore in the film *A League of Their Own,* which he had purchased for $9,000 in 1992.

As at July 2006, McFarlane's assets had a book value of $1,255,187, but an estimated liquidation value of $248,017.

McFarlane owns all the original art that he drew for the *Spawn* series. Nowhere in his assets did McFarlane list this artwork. This was due to the art belonging to Todd McFarlane personally, and not Todd McFarlane Productions. At the time, McFarlane's personal wealth was valued at in excess of $75,000,000, so Todd McFarlane, the individual, was far from destitute.

Assets & Liabilities 2005

It got slightly better for Todd McFarlane Productions. In January 2005, the United States Bankruptcy Court finally got a formal Asset/Liability list from the company.

The assets amounted to $1,565,199 in total. This was made up of $50,722 cash in hand, $345.309 in security deposits for legal retainers, $219,550 for, "Collectible baseballs. The debtor also has a property interest in other miscellaneous items depicting characters and/or events relating to the comic and entertainment businesses whose value is unknown such as posters and other memorabilia. Located in premises," $176,720 in royalties due, $764,266 in claims against insurance companies, the infamous *Spawnmobile,* now worth $7,310, a computer valued at $180 and warehouse shelving valued at $1,092.

The list of creditors was damning.

Stephen A. McConnell: $500,000 for a secured debt. The loan, taken out in November 2004, was against the following, "Accounts receivable including all replacements, renewals and extensions of the Collateral, additions and accessions, proceeds of every kind, every right in proceeds of insurance and related books and records."

Angel Medina: $3,960, Anna Brooks: $1,000, Atwell, Curtis & Brooks, Ltd: $8,399 – a collection agency, Brian Haberlin: $13,600, Brian Holguin: $8,800, Comicraft: $2,200, Danny Miki: $4,440, Greg Capullo: $18,250, Greg Scott: $1,750, Jay Fotos: $5,600, Kim Kolomyjec: $1,560, McFarlane Toys, Inc: $703,688 (an intercompany debt), Register of Copyrights: $60, Tom Orzechowski: $2,200 and Tony Twist: $15,000,000.

In total, McFarlane Productions had liabilities of $16,275,507.

Neil Gaiman was added to that list for an unknown amount.

On the positive side, McFarlane was doing his best to pay as many people as possible. He had reduced debts and/or made payments to Comicraft, Greg Scott and Chance Wolf, along with hundreds of thousands to various lawyers. He was also meeting his payroll obligations, paying a total of $71,455 to his stable of artists and writers from the end of September to the end of November 2004.

This was not a good time to be Todd McFarlane, although you'd barely know it from his public persona. He kept up a brave face, kept giving interviews and talking up *Spawn* along with his sporting hobbies.

Who Owned What

Copyrights

The key to sorting through McFarlane's bankruptcy came with establishing who owned what, especially when it came to copyrights on his various books, both comic books and trade paperbacks. As best as can be established, this is how the copyright ownership looked for characters and books, as of January 2005.

Angela Owned by Todd McFarlane Productions, Inc. and/or Todd McFarlane. This was in dispute, pending the Gaiman case.

Blood Feud Owned by Todd McFarlane Productions, Inc. and/or Todd McFarlane.

Boof and the Bruise Crew. Owned by Todd McFarlane Productions, Inc. and/or Todd McFarlane.

Book of Souls. Owned by Todd McFarlane Productions, Inc. and/or Todd McFarlane.

Case Files: **Sam & Twitch**. Owned by Todd McFarlane Productions, Inc.

Curse of the Spawn Owned by Todd McFarlane Productions, Inc.

Cy-Gor Owned by Todd McFarlane Productions, Inc.

Hell Spawn Owned by Todd McFarlane Productions, Inc. and/or Todd McFarlane.

Kiss – Psycho Circus Copyright owned by Todd McFarlane Productions, Inc. and/or Todd McFarlane. The *Kiss – Psycho Circus* trademark was owned solely by Kiss Catalog Ltd, who had engaged Todd McFarlane Productions on a work-for-hire basis.

Miracleman Owned by Todd McFarlane Productions, Inc, but in dispute.

Ozzy Magazine Boof Owned by Todd McFarlane Productions, Inc. and/or Todd McFarlane.

Sam & Twitch Owned by Todd McFarlane Productions, Inc.

Spawn Owned by Todd McFarlane and/or Todd McFarlane Productions, Inc for the first 78 issues.

Spawn Owned by Todd McFarlane Productions, Inc from issue 79 onwards.

Spawn Simony Owned by Todd McFarlane Productions, Inc.

Spawn Bible Owned by Todd McFarlane Productions, Inc.

Spawn: Blood and Shadows Owned by Todd McFarlane Productions, Inc.

Spawn Impaler Owned by Todd McFarlane Productions, Inc. and/or Todd McFarlane.

Spawn Movie Adaptation Owned by Todd McFarlane Productions, Inc.

Spawn Undead Owned by Todd McFarlane Productions, Inc.

Spawn The Dark Ages Owned by Todd McFarlane Productions, Inc.

Violator Owned by Todd McFarlane Productions, Inc. and/or Todd McFarlane.

Trademarks

The Trademarks weren't as complicated as McFarlane had registered, or assigned, them all under the Todd McFarlane Productions umbrella. These now included

Angela (Reg. No. 2,252,303)

Curse of the Spawn (Reg. No. 2,251,056)

Eclipse Comics (Reg. No. 1,448,449)

McFarlane Toys (Reg. No. 2,904,096)

McFarlane's Evil Prophecy (Reg. No, 3,181,317)

Medieval Spawn (Reg. No. 2,027,972)

Spawn (Reg. No. 3,020,406)

Spawn Alley (Reg. No. 2,031,270)

Spawn Mobile (Reg. No. 2,045,164)

the Spawn Image Logo (Reg. No. 1,793,662)

the Spawn Logo (Reg. No. 1,817,902)

Tremor (Reg. No. 2,100,447)

Violator (Reg. No. 2,027,968)

In addition to this list, McFarlane, via his companies, had filed for trademarks on the following and, at the time of the bankruptcy, they were in limbo. Each one of these applications would ultimately be abandoned by McFarlane.

Circular Design Horz

Clown

Manga Spawn

Miracleman

Ninja Spawn

Spawn in Chinese

the Spawn movie title

Violator Monster Rig

McFarlane Productions also held trademarks in Europe, China, Hong Kong, Canada, Japan and Taiwan.

Naturally the ownership of these copyrights and trademarks, in particular *Miracleman,* which was being opposed by Gaiman, were now in dispute with the

Gaiman case.

It was in McFarlane's best interests to settle with as many of his creditors as possible before the courts were forced to intervene and start stripping him of his trademarks and copyrights. If this didn't happen then McFarlane was in real danger of losing *Spawn.* It wouldn't be a voluntary move, the court could order that the assets be sold at auction, ala Eclipse, to resolve the debts.

But there was a lot to happen before things reached that stage, and there was no way known that McFarlane was going to lose his baby.

Settlements

As September 2006, came around settlements continued to happen. First up was Travelers, who offered to settle with McFarlane for a one-off payment of $615,000 for defense costs incurred in the Twist case. After monies were distributed, McFarlane was left with $285,359 sitting in an account earning interest, but untouchable for him.

Next was Tony Twist.

McFarlane's lawyers finally settled with Tony Twist in 2007 after the Missouri Court of Appeals denied McFarlane's motion for yet another rehearing. The settlement wasn't as simple as it could have been, with Hanover, General Star and Citizens combining to pay McFarlane an indemnity payment of $5,000,000, which was handed to Twist as a full and final settlement.

Twist's $5,000,000 was broken down as follows:

> $433,686.11 payable to Blitz, Bardgett & Deutsch, LC, representing reimbursement for its expenses incurred in the Twist Litigation, Insurance Litigation and related matters.
>
> $333,333.40 payable to Blitz, Bardgett & Deutsch, LC, representing the

difference between the 40% contingency agreement of Twist with BBD and the 33 1/3% contingency agreement with Twist asserted by Riezman Berger, P.C.

$1,666,666.60 payable to Blitz, Bardgett & Deutsch, LC, and Riezman Berger, P.C., jointly, representing the balance of attorneys' fees) and to be placed in an escrow account with Regions Bank in St. Louis, Missouri, pending an agreement by Blitz, Bardgett & Deutsch, LC, and Riezman Berger, P.C. regarding division thereof or determination of same by a Missouri Court.

$2,566,313.89 payable to Tony Twist and Jocelyn Twist, jointly, and to be placed in an escrow account with Regions Bank in St. Louis, Missouri, to be distributed pursuant to prior agreement of Twist and Jocelyn Twist.

In accepting the settlement, Blitz, Bardgett & Deutsch also lifted the garnishment that had been placed upon Todd McFarlane Productions, Todd McFarlane and Wanda Kolomyjec.

Twist was also required to tell the court that he was satisfied with the settlement and thus had no further claim against McFarlane or his insurance companies

Twist finally signed the settlement on 11 January 2007, closing the chapter that began the entire saga. It was far removed from the original $24,000,000 judgement and even the $15,000,000 that the court later awarded to Twist, but it wasn't chump change by anyone's standards. At the end of the more than ten-year fight, Twist ended up with just over $2,500,000.

In a win for McFarlane, he had his personal bank accounts back.

The settlement with Twist gave McFarlane more breathing space, as the claims had represented $18,000,000 of the total debt originally claimed. He had cleared the decks of Tony Twist and the insurance companies.

Another major settlement happened in 2008. In March 2004 TMP had entered into a Memorandum of Agreement (MOA) with DPS Film Roman Inc. to produce a new series of the Animated *Spawn* television show. HBO still held the rights to the original *Spawn* series, but any new show developed after January 1, 2004, would be controlled by TMP. As such McFarlane had prepared concepts and designs and found an interested party to co-produce and distribute the show.

The MOA called for TMP to provide the services of McFarlane and Terry Fitzgerald, with Film Roman to provide the rest. Film Roman would provide the funding for the series, and it was intended to be a direct to video production. The profit cut would be 70% to TMP and 30% to Film Roman, along with TMP being paid $15,000 in royalties for each hour-long show, and McFarlane pocketing an additional $10,000 for each show, plus bonuses if the show was picked up for television syndication[1]. If all went well, the amount McFarlane could earn for every hour of Animated *Spawn* was $25,000 as a starting point, going as high as $37,500. McFarlane was responsible for paying Fitzgerald out of his end.

The contract was signed on 34 March 2004. In December, TMP filed for Chapter 11, meaning its assets, including the Film Roman agreement, were uncertain.

With this uncertainty, and unable to mount a valid production, Film Roman decided to sell the purchased asset (Spawn Animated). Film Roman had invested $1,113,964 to date, with another $554,244 still outstanding.

McFarlane wanted to buy Film Roman out, if only to keep *Spawn* out of third-party hands. However, as TMP was in Chapter 11, he would have to petition the court for permission. This was done and, ultimately, permission was refused. In response McFarlane, via a new company, Todd McFarlane Entertainment Inc, made a pitch to buy the show back. This would cost McFarlane $700,000 cash, $350,000 payable upon approval of the order and the remainder upon the closing of the order. McFarlane would now be liable for the costs outstanding from the Film Roman production ($554,244) and the costs of any contracts. In return McFarlane would inherit the entire production, all contracts, all items – lock, stock and barrel. This would leave McFarlane to find another $554,244 to pay off the liabilities, and Film Roman were now out $413,964 from their production costs. Still, it was another creditor paid and, along the way, McFarlane had managed to regain a part of *Spawn*.

All that remained was Neil Gaiman.

.

Gaiman Wins A Miracle(Man)

"I was hoping that there may be a wild card in the deck called *Miracleman* that may or may not have some value, and so if we sort of hit some snag where we couldn't resolve some of the issues that maybe there is a sort of a more non-traditional way to resolve it by going let's do a character swap or a hostage swapping, if you will, you know, of some of the characters. And so *Miracleman* potentially became that.[1]" – Todd McFarlane

Eventually McFarlane would lose, again, to Gaiman as well, costing him another seven-figure sum along with *Miracleman*.

As late as 2009 McFarlane was still, in public at least, insisting that he owned *Miracleman*.

In the interim, Marvel Comics had done a deal with Mick Anglo and bought *Marvelman*, registering the trademark on 24 July 2009. As far as they were concerned, they were halfway home. They had Gaiman on side and now they had *Marvelman*. Marvel began to reprint the classic Anglo stories, with new covers from the likes of Joe Quesada.

McFarlane was realistic about the whole situation. "As you might imagine, that character has been a much talked about topic of conversation, even involved to some degree in the lawsuit with myself and Neil. It's a curious topic. I can't profess to have all the answers on it, so again I'd be sort of foolish to speak out of school. Obviously Marvel believes they have certain rights to it. I know that I and my lawyers believe we have certain rights. The question is just what can we do to settle it and when can we settle it. One way would be for someone to just give up and say it's not worth it. The other way would be to sit down and have a meaningful conversation like gentlemen, to find a way so that everyone can win. Not necessarily so either party can win, but for the comic community to win. To figure out a way to get this character back out there and not be a pain in the ass to the point where people have to look over their shoulder.

"Every party involved has a position that they feel they are entitled to with the character. That would include Marvel, Neil, it and myself. I think the prudent thing would be to see if there can't be an adult conversation to be had instead of rubbing people's noses in it.[2]"

Gaiman had become aware of new characters in the *Spawn* universe, *Lord Covenant*, the lead character of *Spawn: The Dark Ages*. Two new angels had been introduced into *Spawn,* called *Tiffany* and *Domina* essentially taking the place of *Angela,* who McFarlane and writer Brian Holguin had killed off in *Spawn* #100. Gaiman believed that the two new angels were derivative of *Angela* and, as such, he wanted to be paid.

With this in mind, McFarlane elected to roll the dice and asked that the case go back to trial. Before this could happen, the presiding magistrate decided to instead hold a motion hearing to see if there was enough in the case to head to a full jury trial.

The motion hearing was held on 14 June 2010.

Although a new character, created by writer Brian Holguin, Gaiman felt *Lord Covenant* was his *Medieval Spawn* under a different name, and the two angels were substitute for *Angela*. For Gaiman, these were not new characters, rather they were derivative characters. As such he was now asking for a slice of the profits on these three characters, as well as *Angela, Medieval Spawn* and the other characters from *Spawn* #9.

Holguin had written *Spawn* and *Kiss: Psycho Circus* before being handed *Spawn: The Dark Ages*, which he wrote the first 14 issues. He told the court how he came to create *Lord Covenant*.

"Concurrently with writing *Dark Ages*, I was writing, as I said, the flagship title, the main *Spawn* book. And I believe I started around Issue 70, which is quite a few years after, you know, Issue 9, the issues you had been talking about earlier. And one of the things I wanted to do was to expand the Spawn Universe and look at the themes that were explored in the main book and explore them further in the context of the new book, and so the character of *Lord Covenant* had many psychological and emotional similarities to Al Simmons as well as having differences.

"Al Simmons, one of the things that intrigued me about him was the character is essentially a good man. He is a loving husband, good neighbor, but he is also a paid assassin. He is a government contract killer. And his rationale is that, well, I'm only killing the bad people. And if they didn't send me -- you know, there is a reason they are sending me after these people, and this is a reason why he is condemned to Hell and finds himself being a *Hellspawn*.

"Similarly, *Lord Covenant* was a killer for what he thought was a good reason. He joined the Crusades. He believed it was his religious duty to travel over to the Holy Land and kill infidels. And when he dies, there is a scene in there, and probably the most dramatic scene in the first issue, where he is fully expecting to go to Heaven to be rewarded for all the people he has murdered and is somewhat shocked to find himself in Hell and facing the same deal that Al Simmons would be faced with hundreds of years later.[3]"

Holguin told the court that he did not base *Lord Covenant* on *Medieval Spawn*.

Nor was he aware of the Alan Moore convention that there could be only one *Spawn* every 400 years. As Holguin said, "When I started off Spawn, Todd kind of talked me through the rules, the rules of his universe, the rules of his creation. And I read some of the back issues and a lot of them he said, "Forget about this stuff. This is what I want you to concentrate on.[4]"

McFarlane was even more direct about the alleged similarities between *Medieval Spawn* and *Lord Covenant*.

"If the intent was for me to do a *Medieval Spawn* comic book," he told the court, "a couple things would have happened: It would have been called *Medieval Spawn*, sort of easy stuff; It would have looked like *Medieval Spawn*; and We would have just sort of led to any components, of which there weren't a lot, from Issues 9 and 14 and 50 to go. That wasn't the intent. It's not because we were trying to be devious, because there is a more obvious answer, because we weren't trying to do that. And so Issue 14 and 15 was me replicating something that I had seen before, which is Issue 9. *Dark Ages Spawn* wasn't replicating that because we could have made it look like that. Liam Sharp is a tremendously skilled artist. He could have made it look like, quote/unquote, *Medieval Spawn*; he didn't. We came up with another character with another look based on the components and the mechanisms of the original pre-existing *Spawn* and all the backstories on him.[5]"

McFarlane's explanations aside, the court found that *Dark Ages Spawn* was a derivate of *Medieval Spawn*. *Tiffany* and *Domina* were 'mere variations of the *Angela* character,' and thus were also derivative. McFarlane was ordered to provide accounting for the three characters. Now Gaiman was looking at owning, or at least co-owning, *Medieval Spawn, Cogliostro, Angela, Lord Covenant, Tiffany* and, *Domina*. It appeared that each time McFarlane found himself in court with Gaiman, he came away handing more of his properties over.

Behind the scenes negotiations were taking place. Gaiman quietly surrendered his rights to *Medieval Spawn* and *Cogliostro* in exchange for McFarlane's rights in *Angela*. This was a win-win for both parties as McFarlane had 'killed off' *Angela* and had no further use for the character. Gaiman also had no use for co-ownership of *Spawn* related characters that, in all possibility, would never see print again.

Miracleman would take a bit more effort. With the impending closure of the civil court case, Gaiman made it known that he would now shift his attention of the trademark opposition against McFarlane. This opposition could see McFarlane tied to the courts for years to come and remain in Chapter 11 for the foreseeable future. As both sides now wanted to finally end the legal battles, a solution was reached. Gaiman would give up any claims for *Dark Ages Spawn, Tiffany* and *Domina* in a straight swap for McFarlane's claims to *Miracleman*.

All that remained was to finally account for the money.

After more negotiations between the lawyers a settlement agreement was drafted and, after considering all the issues, the court made its final judgment.

> IT IS ORDERED AND ADJUDGED that judgment is entered in favor of plaintiffs and against the McFarlane defendants declaring that plaintiff Neil Gaiman is a joint 50% owner of the copyrights to the publications

> *Spawn* issues 9 and 26 and *Angela* issues 1, 2 and 3 and the content of those publications, with the respective future rights and obligations of the parties with respect hereto being resolved under the terms of their settlement agreement.
>
> IT IS FURTHER ORDERED AND ADJUDGED that judgment is entered dismissing all remaining claims and counterclaims with prejudice[6], the parties having waived in their settlement agreement any right of appeal with respect to any such claims or counterclaims. All parties are to bear their own attorney fees and costs[7].

With that proclamation, the case that had run for a decade was now finally closed forever. This also removed the last of the debtors for McFarlane, which meant he could now close out his bankruptcy once and for all. $382,000 that had been placed in escrow in 2004 was duly released, plus interest, and handed to Gaiman, who donated the lot to comic book related charities.

After all the legal blustering, on both sides of the fence, the issue of who owned *Miracleman* never actually went to court. Instead it sat in the background, to be used as the ultimate bargaining chip by both Neil Gaiman and Todd McFarlane. As Gaiman took more and more of the *Spawn* universe with him, even half ownership, McFarlane saw the logic in handing over what Gaiman really wanted – *Miracleman* – and getting back what he really wanted – *Spawn* - the universe that he believed he had created alone.

Not that McFarlane owns the entire *Spawn* universe. He is no longer able to issue a complete library of *Spawn* comics without consulting, and obtaining the permission from, Gaiman. This includes *Spawn* issues 9 and 26. Nor can he reprint the *Angela* mini-series. On the other hand, if Gaiman wanted to reprint that material, he, too, would be forced to deal with McFarlane. This has been resolved, to a degree. Early editions of *Spawn* trade paperback reprints often omitted issues 9 and 10 (featuring Dave Sim's *Cerebus*), but, as of 2009's *Spawn Origins*, both issues were included, which would mean Gaiman and Sim have come to legal terms with McFarlane and allowed the reprinting of their work.

Gaiman took *Miracleman* and *Angela* to the Marvel Universe. Marvel now owned *Marvelman* and *Miracleman. Angela* was a bonus, but one that they would be quick to exploit. If these losses did bother McFarlane, he never said anything about it in public. He took it head on and, publicly at least, shrugged his shoulders and moved forward.

"Neil Gaiman and I had a resolution in our legal dispute, and as part of that he ended up with the rights of *Angela*. Whatever Neil chooses to do with something that he owns is at his complete and utter discretion. The health of the industry is based upon having good stories and good characters, and a wide customer base. If bringing some of these characters back to the fold in a meaningful way adds to that, then it just strengthens our industry.[8]"

McFarlane v Spawn

> "*Superman* is Clark Kent. *Spider-Man* is Peter Parker. *Spawn* is Al Simmons...[1]"

Or was he?

By 2012 it would have been a fair assumption that Todd McFarlane was sick of being in court. However one thing that people should have learnt was that McFarlane would go to any length to protect his creation, *Spawn*.

While McFarlane has shown he has no issue with fans drawing his characters, he does draw a line when it comes to people attempting to profit from them. Just how far was about to be shown to the world at large.

Spawn was being used and this time it was McFarlane on the offensive as he brought suit against one of his oldest friends and close confidant in the form of *Spawn* namesake Al Simmons.

As a McFarlane employee Al Simmons had been cashing in on his connection with McFarlane since the beginnings of *Spawn*. The two had met in college where they were roommates. They also had another shared passion in the form of baseball. McFarlane was a decent ballplayer. He had been playing centerfield since he was a child, generally on Little League teams coached by his father, Bobby, and managed by his future father-in-law Morley Kolomyjec. He showed enough potential to be given a tryout with Gonzaga University and he attended Eastern Washington University on a baseball scholarship. He finally got a shot at the big time when the Toronto Blue Jays invited him to try out but, sadly, he ended up finishing last on the roster. That was the end of McFarlane's baseball dream.

The baseball career of Al Simmons ran parallel with McFarlane's, but he managed to get one step closer than McFarlane to the Major leagues after he was drafted, albeit to the minor league system, by the San Diego Padres in 1982. An injury would see him cut from the Padre's roster and he settled himself for a career working for the government.

The two men remained in touch over the years, and when Image began in 1992, the first people McFarlane hired to assist him with his new business ventures were his friends, Al Simmons and Terry Fitzgerald. He also named two significant characters in *Spawn* after them. *Spawn*'s alter ego was Al Simmons. *Spawns* best friend was Terry Fitzgerald. Simmons wife, Melanie, was quickly hired by McFarlane to head up the HR department for his companies.

McFarlane liked to keep as much as possible in house.

There was another bonus to having Al Simmons on the books. Al was still in shape and an African-American, same as *Spawn*. It made perfect sense to fit the real life Simmons up with a *Spawn* costume and have him appear as, well, the real life *Spawn,* aka Al Simmons.

It was a perfect marketing idea and one that McFarlane leapt upon that would unfortunately lead to some issues.

As the years went on, Simmons began to immerse himself deeper into the role of being, well, Al Simmons, aka *Spawn*. He would sign copies of *Spawn* comics with those words, "Al Simmons, aka *Spawn*". Simmons immersed himself deeper and deeper into the role and made more and more public appearances in costume until McFarlane decided to scale it back.

In 2011 Simmons approached McFarlane with the idea of publishing his own autobiography. McFarlane questioned the idea but agreed to assist as long as Simmons didn't reveal any corporate secrets or, worse still, attempt to claim he was *Spawn*. McFarlane wanted the book to be accurate and honest. Simmons agreed.

As blissfully ignorant that McFarlane might appear, he was guided by others who knew better, including Simmons wife, Melanie.

As the head of Human Resources for Todd McFarlane Productions International (TMPI), it was Melanie Simmons duty to ensure that all employees, including Al Simmons, were aware of their obligations to the various McFarlane companies. This included the signing of both Confidentiality and Non-Disclosure Agreements (NDA) which would remain in effect after they'd left McFarlane's employ.

The agreements stated, among other things, that all employees would;

> (1) not to use or disclose the McFarlane Companies' business information, including products, sources, costs of products, or any other information, during their employment and after employment terminates;
>
> (2) not to use unpublished or copyrighted materials;
>
> (3) to maintain confidentiality concerning the McFarlane Companies and McFarlane.

During a pre-arranged interview for the book, McFarlane once again reiterated his stance on the book. It would not be endorsed by McFarlane, would not be published by Image and McFarlane would not allow the use of *Spawn* in the title. Furthermore, McFarlane wanted it to be clear that Simmons not take any credit for the character or reveal any of the company secrets.

Simmons again reassured McFarlane that the book would be about him, Al Simmons.

The book certainly had its issues, not the least that it appeared to be written by a person with very little knowledge of McFarlane's career in the comic book world. Just a read of one section would have been enough for McFarlane.

"He (McFarlane), meanwhile, became a shining star, moving up into the rarefied air of being the world's most successful and celebrated illustrator/writer of comic book epics, and not just any comic books. He was published by both publishing powerhouses, Marvel and D.C. Comics. There, he did no less than oversee a rebirth and update of the superheroes of decades past, taking Batman and Spider-man from outdated, near-irrelevant status to modern-day sainthood. He reworked these heroes obsessed not so much with superhuman strength but superhuman wits and cunning. Rather than flat and old fashioned, Todd created characters who also possessed a modern sensibility, with real -life inner conflicts that forced them to dig down deep inside their own souls for the answers to surviving the Armageddon that arose in each new issue, in each new challenge to the free world. It was daring; it was raw. The images burned with a new intensity and flare. The caped crusader and the human spider suddenly were more than muscled comic book clichés. They had flesh, they had blood, and they had an ambivalent reluctance about what they were doing.[2]"

There are several problems with the above statements. First and foremost, McFarlane never wrote an issue of *Batman*. Before he formed Image, he had drawn three issues of *Detective Comics*, and that only came about after Alan Davis and Paul Neary left the title mid-story. Even the subsequent *Spawn/Batman* crossover that he produced was written by Frank Miller.

And McFarlane himself knew, and had admitted, that his writing on the *Spider-Man* title was anything but groundbreaking. The rest was hyperbole at its most extreme.

Other statements in the book included a claim that the *Batman* and *Spider-Man* movies that had been issued to that date, including the original 1989 Michael Keaton *Batman* film, were part of McFarlane's legacy along with the previously mentioned, and repeated several times, claim that *Spawn* was the first African-American super hero. Most damning, for McFarlane, was a claim that McFarlane was at a cross-road when he formed Image and that failure would have rendered him irrelevant and washed up.

This last claim would fire the self-made McFarlane up more than anything else. To be labeled as a man desperate for success at the cost of being redundant, angered him. But then Simmons compounded his mistakes by attempting to claim part of *Spawn*. If anyone had learnt anything over the years, it was McFarlane whom, rightly, considered himself the sole creator of *Spawn*. He would not allow anyone to take any credit for any aspect of the character, no matter how minor or, in this case, major.

McFarlane only ever said that he named *Spawn* after Simmons. *Spawn* could have easily been called Jim Salicrup[3] or Erik Larsen had McFarlane looked elsewhere the day he named him.

For his part, Simmons saw things differently. A lot differently.

"When Todd told me he wanted to use the name Al Simmons as *Spawn's* alter ego identity, it was, of course, a high honor, the ultimate flattery," Simmons would write in the introduction to his book, *The Art of Being Spawn*. "For Todd, the project was the ultimate dare: *Spawn* would be the most eagerly awaited new comic book in eons; and it would be Todd's first under his Image Comics label. Of no small importance, it would also introduce the first African -American comic book superhero to the masses.[4]"

Unfortunately for Simmons, there were several things wrong with that single paragraph. African-American superheroes had been around since the 1960s when Stan Lee and artist Gene Colan introduced *The Falcon* to the public via the pages of *Captain America*[5]. Since then several African American superheroes had appeared in the pages of both marvel and DC, and a host of smaller publishers. Marvel had *Blade, Luke Cage (Power Man), Storm (X-Men), Black Goliath, Deathlok, Misty Knight* and more. DC had *Black Lightning, Black Racer, Tyroc, Vixen* amongst others. At various smaller publishers was *Sabre* and *Megaton* and other minor characters. As good as *Spawn* was as a character, it wasn't a first.

And Todd McFarlane knew that. He never once stated that *Spawn* was the first African-American superhero.

As the book rolled on, Simmons continued to take credit for the success of *Spawn*. To the casual reader it appeared that McFarlane and Simmons had collaborated on *Spawn*, on both the marketing and creation.

"*Spawn* brought us together as a team, by giving life and animation to the most unforgettable character in comic book history. True, there was a certain symmetry between *Spawn* and the real Al Simmons.[6]"

Adding to the damage was the book's title, *The Art of Being Spawn*. The front cover showed Simmons in a *Spawn* costume, with a *Spawn* mask, featuring a *Spawn* logo and with McFarlane's name prominently positioned.

Already being advertised on-line, the book's authors were listed as Al Simmons and Todd McFarlane and the proposed publisher was none other than Image Comics. It would appear to the casual reader that this was, indeed, a book about *Spawn* co-written and officially endorsed by Todd McFarlane, which was exactly what McFarlane had wanted to avoid.

In 2012 the book was ready to be published and was being advertised on-line via

Amazon. A pre-publication copy found its way to McFarlane who, upon reading, or, at least skimming, it, alerted Simmons to the problems that he had with the book. McFarlane demanded that the book be placed on hold until a solution could be worked out. Failing that, the book would simply have to be pulped.

Simmons responded that the book was about to be released. Indeed, he had started to promote it with a web-site and had made himself available for interviews. In short, it was too late for anyone to do anything about the book, not that Simmons was inclined to do so.

Too late for anyone to do anything, except for Todd McFarlane. The next time he contacted Simmons he was no longer Toddy, old baseball pal, now he was Todd McFarlane, angry, very angry.

McFarlane then promptly sacked both Al and Melanie Simmons. He asked, one last time, for the book to be cancelled and withdrawn. Simmons again refused, calling McFarlane's bluff.

That wasn't the best course of action as McFarlane promptly brought suit against both Al and Melanie Simmons.

According to McFarlane's complaint the book was nothing short of a betrayal. The complaint stated that the book was;

> "...riddled with knowing untruths, inaccuracies, misappropriations of the McFarlane Companies' trade secrets, disclosures of the McFarlane Companies' and McFarlane's confidential information, and infringements on the McFarlane Companies' and McFarlane's intellectual property rights.
>
> "One of the most egregious examples of false and misleading information in the Book is Al Simmons' suggestion in the Book that his life was allegedly the inspiration for or provided any background for the "Spawn" character. Al Simmons, who was flattered and eagerly gave his consent to McFarlane in 1992 for his name to be a part of "Spawn," was not the inspiration for "Spawn's" central character and no one has ever confused that character with Defendant Al Simmons. Curiously, Defendant Al Simmons has, over the years, as "Spawn" enjoyed popularity, remarked on how his association with Plaintiffs has provided him with some name recognition or notoriety, where he had none before "Spawn." Defendant Simmons has, in effect, traded on Plaintiffs' fame, brand and copyright protected creation, and

> now is deliberately using falsities in the Book to further attempt to improperly capitalize and infringe upon the McFarlane Companies' property interests and McFarlane's name, likeness and identity.[7]"

The book had used McFarlane's name and likeness on the cover and boasted that it had been written, "...with contributions by *Spawn* Creator Todd McFarlane". Adding to the damage were the advertising blurbs which, in addition to using McFarlane's name and likeness, and also the *Spawn* logo and costume, claimed; "Todd McFarlane named Al... as the alter ego of the *Spawn* character," and "Al and Todd have lived nearly parallel lives."

McFarlane asked for the book to be withdrawn from sale, same as he'd asked Simmons in private. Now he also wanted all sold copies recalled and $75,000 in estimated damages. He claimed his privacy had been violated, that his name was being used to endorse the book against his wishes and that the *Spawn* trademark had been infringed.

If anyone was gearing up for another protracted court case, they were to be highly disappointed. Simmons capitulated immediately without filing a defense. Simmons knew he couldn't fight McFarlane on a financial level and, having seen how McFarlane fought his legal case via litigation and appeals, he accepted a deal. The deal involved the withdrawal of the book[8] and an undisclosed amount of damages. The case had been filed at the end of September 2011, and by the first week of December, it was all over.

With this settlement, which was never disclosed to the court or the public, and for once to his advantage, McFarlane drew a close on his legal battles.

In The End, Who Really Won?

When all the dust settled and with the benefit of hindsight, it's clear that not everyone came out of the cases clear victors.

Tony Twist won but he never got his $24,000,000. In fact, he got a fraction of that amount. He never fully recovered from the motorcycle accident in 1999 and retired that year from ice hockey and is now considered to be a legend, a thug or a boogeyman, depending on who you speak to.

Neil Gaiman won. He donated the money he was awarded from McFarlane to comic book charities and traded the derivate *Spawn* characters that he was given 50% ownership of for 100% of *Miracleman* and *Angela*. He promptly sold those characters to Marvel Comics. When not writing books and films, he likes to travel the world doing spoken word tours and secretly signing any books of his at airport bookstores.

Thanks to Gaiman, *Miracleman, Marvelman* and *Angela* are now part of the Marvel Universe. This also means that Gaiman and artist Mark Buckingham are working to finally finish their *Miracleman* trilogy.

Spawn and all the derivate Spawn characters, such as *Medieval Spawn,* are still with McFarlane. Officially McFarlane has three children, Jake, Cyan and Kate. It can easily be argued that he has a fourth child named *Spawn.*

Neither Rob Liefeld nor Image Comics won their case. Liefeld and the Image partners eventually buried several hatchets and reunited for their twentieth anniversary. McFarlane continued the renewed friendship by having Liefeld draw a variant cover for *Spawn* #200, as well as interiors of *Spawn* #196 which McFarlane inked. Just like the old days.

The original Image creators then announced a new series, titled *Image United*, which would celebrate the anniversary. Written by Robert Kirkman (Walking Dead), the book would be drawn by Portacio, Liefeld, Silvestri, McFarlane, Larsen and Valentino with covers by Jim Lee. Each artist would draw their respective characters and the series was slated for six issues. The first two issues appeared, on time, in 2009, the third in August 2010 and, as of 2019, that was it. When asked about the delay, Larsen and Silvestri were diplomatic and skirted the issue by sharing the blame. Liefeld, however, placed the blame squarely on the shoulders of McFarlane. Just like the old days.

A number of lawyers and legal firms won. They billed all the parties involved for amounts running into the millions of dollars over the decade and a half of legal action.

Cat Yronwode writes and edits books and sits on the board of Yronwode Institution for the Preservation and Popularization of Indigenous Ethnomagicology (YIPPIE). She is active in preserving the culture of 19th and 20th century folk magic and divination. Since 2006, she has been a pastor at Missionary Independent Spiritual Church.

Dean Mullaney now works as a creative director at IDW Publishing, Jan Mullaney went back to making music.

Alan Moore still writes and is still Alan Moore.

Gareb Shamus runs the Wizard World conventions. He now describes himself as an American contemporary painter and is part of New York's emerging Connectivism movement. His artworks have been exhibited around the globe.

Alan Davis won. He finally got paid for his *Miracleman* work when Marvel began to reprint it. He proved that bygones could indeed be bygones when he contributed new covers to the series and provided scans of his art. He writes and draws for both Marvel and DC Comics.

As forTodd McFarlane... he lost, and also won. He took his hits and is still going strong. As always, people love him or hate him. He'd be used to that; he's been that way since he took over art chores on the *Amazing Spider-Man*.

In 1993 McFarlane summed himself up. "Rob Liefeld and Todd McFarlane... probably the two most despised men on the planet of comic books. And you know what? We're still having a ball in our lives, because the people who hate us, we don't give a crap about, because I'm writing a comic book for fifteen to sixteen-year-old kids and some grand poo-bah who's 42 years old decides he didn't like the *Spawn*. Well, you know what? It's like building a tricycle and having some adult say, 'It sucks, it doesn't fit me.' Well, it's a tricycle, for God's sake! So criticism... my mom doesn't like everything I do, my wife doesn't like everything I do. So, if I can still live with the fact that my wife doesn't like everything I do, I could really care less whether John Byrne likes it, you know?[1]"

Those words still fit the man over twenty-five years later.

And Then...

"It's nice to be back doing steady comic book work. I sorta took a side step away from that when I was running my other businesses. Coming back to do some writing and drawing and inking on a regular basis is very therapeutic. After running big corporations, if you will, you just lock yourself in a room, all by yourself, and not have to have any meetings, or deal with bankers and government regulations, and some of the other stuff that I had to deal with my other company. It's been good for me, at least mentally. People have said to me, "You ought to come back and draw books on a regular basis." The answer might be yes, but if I ever do that it will be because I just want to draw again. It's good for me mentally. It would be way, way, way less about whether the book is a top seller or if we win awards or if I get any critical acclaim. I've run that gamut already in my life. At least for me, now that I've had my 15 minutes of fame, those aren't the motivating factors as I go forward with stuff. I want to do things that make life enjoyable. Maybe I'll come back and I'll do a book about frogs for all I know. I'd want to do something that keeps my interest. I don't care if everybody's buying it because I made a good living and saved money in the bank. I just like drawing, which is different than going, "I need to put this character in there and that character in there." There's a bit on an unintentional manipulation when you're running a business trying to maximize sales all the time. Sometimes you paint yourself into corners

> where creatively you might not otherwise go. It's been good and luckily, I've hung around.[1]" – Todd McFarlane

Amazingly, after all of his problems, Todd McFarlane is still going strong and is still a powerhouse in the comic book industry. Even more incredibly, after nearly thirty years, he's still publishing *Spawn.* Every so often he writes an issue and keeps his hand in with the artwork. And good on him.

He's made mistakes over the years, mainly due to his own hubris, and yet he's prevailed after defeat and keeps on being, well, Todd McFarlane. He's made, and lost, millions of dollars during his illustrious career, and he continues to move forward, announcing a new *Spawn* movie and setting up yet another new company, McFarlane Films, LLC (as of August 2017). Slated to star Academy Award winner Jamie Foxx as *Spawn* and Jeremy 'Hawkeye' Renner, the untitled film will see McFarlane working as co-director, co-producer and writer, taking on a similar role that Frank Miller did with his *Sin City* film.

McFarlane is promising to deliver the most brutal comic book movie ever made. Unlike the 1997 New Line Cinema effort, McFarlane is keeping both hands firmly on the wheel.

It would have been easy, and highly tempting, for McFarlane to have given up on *Spawn* during those dark days of 1998 to 2012 and simply gone back to either Marvel or DC. Other Image founders have done it, Liefeld, Larsen, Lee and Silvestri all returned to work for both Marvel and DC – Jim Lee is now Publisher and CCO of DC Comics. Larsen still works for Image and has shown that he can work for both Marvel and Image at the same time. Jim Valentino, like McFarlane, has remained true to Image.

The last Image Comics holdout, Marvel or DC Comics would have accepted a return from Todd McFarlane during his legal battles, no matter his issues with Neil Gaiman, or anyone else, without hesitation. And they still would. If you think otherwise, then you don't understand the cut-throat world of comic book publishing where money talks above all other considerations.

Marvel would have paid handsomely for a new McFarlane drawn *Spider-Man* series and it doesn't take too much imagination to visualize just how much he could have made drawing a Frank Miller scripted *Batman* series at DC – probably more than what Jim Lee earned for his *Batman & Robin* run. It would have been all too easy, but to entertain the thought is to underestimate Todd McFarlane.

To return would have been a step backwards for McFarlane and one he was unwilling to even consider. Plus, he didn't need the money, bankruptcy notwithstanding. If he goes back to either company it will be on his own terms, at a time of his own choosing and not one dictated by circumstance.

Ironically, McFarlane showed that he can move past grudges when he accepted an invitation to participate in a book published by Marvel Comics to raise funds for those affected by 9-11. McFarlane's contribution was to ink, over pencils by Joe Quesada, a figure of a fire-fighter crying. He's also drawn *Spider-Man* in recent times, on sketch covers, mainly to benefit charities such as the Hero Initiative. McFarlane knows the value of his *Spider-Man* and doesn't give it cheaply, but if there's a cause that he believes in then he gives freely.

The longer he stays away from the major companies, the more he's worth to both upon return.

That is, if he ever does decide to return.

Marvel has recently repurposed old McFarlane art, in the same way they did for Jim Lee, for use as variant covers on recent comic books. After nearly thirty years, Marvel are still profiting from McFarlane, and, if his old art is still worthy enough of publishing, his new art would be stellar for them. But, as he's often said, as long as he's the President and CEO of Image Comics, it just isn't going to happen, although he has left the door slightly ajar for a *Spawn/Spider-Man* crossover, saying he'd love to do it. Eventually.

For those keeping score, here's a rundown of the various McFarlane companies as they stand today: McFarlane Collector's Club, Inc., McFarlane Films, LLC, McFarlane Toys, Inc., McFarlane Worldwide, Inc., Todd McFarlane Productions, Inc., TMP International, Inc., Haunt, LLC and McFarlane Stores, LLC.

Also included is his 25% share of Image Comics and an increased number of trademarks (but not *Miracleman*). That's a lot of pies for his fingers.

McFarlane, in his way, inspired many to enter the comic book industry. Similar to how Joe Shuster, Jack Kirby, Mac Raboy and Hal Foster inspired the likes of Curt Swan, John Romita, Steve Ditko and John Buscema, who, in turn, again with Kirby, inspired the likes of John Byrne, George Perez, Rick Vietch and Steve Bissette, who, in turn, inspired the likes of McFarlane, Jim Lee and Rob Liefeld.

He wasn't the worst of his generation, far from it. The story has often been that many artists were told by Stan Lee to draw like Kirby, Steve Ditko or John Romita, a lot of those following McFarlane would be told by their editors and writers to draw like Todd McFarlane.

Many have tried, many have failed. Some, such as Stephen Platt and Greg Capullo, made a mark and quickly developed their own style or faded into obscurity. Most ignored the advice or moved on and found their own style anyway, which should have been the point in the first place.

McFarlane knew a secret that many of his imitators never cottoned onto; McFarlane knew what the kids reading his comics wanted, because, on many levels. They wanted flash, big pictures, gore and heroic superheroes. How McFarlane knew this was easy. He simply never stopped being a kid himself. In so many ways, he never grew up.

"The greatest single value that anybody can give me is freedom. That's it. That's going to be the epitaph when I die. It's just going to say: 'Here lies Todd McFarlane. He was free'. Period.[2]"

Love him or loathe him, there's a lot to admire in Todd McFarlane.

Addendum 1: Angela at Image

From a promising early start through to the end, Angela featured heavily at Image comics. Her first appearance came in *Spawn* #9 (March 1993) and her last appearance in the Image Universe came in *Spawn* #100 (November 2000) with a flashback in *Spawn* #101 (December 2000).

This is a checklist of her Image Universe appearances, complete with who wrote the character.

Angela (Writer: Neil Gaiman)

#1 - Book 1

#2 - Book 2

#3 - Book 3

Angela (Writer: Beau Smith)

#0 - Ocean Of Evil. Vessel Of The Doomed

Angela/Glory: Rage of Angels (Writers: Rob Liefeld and Robert Place Napton)

#1

Aria/Angela (Writer: Brian Holguin)

#1 - Heavenly Creatures

#2 - Heavenly Creatures

Curse of the Spawn (Writer: Alan McElroy)

#9 - Limbo

#10 - A Fall of Doves

#11 - Cataclysm

Glory (Writer: Mary Jo Duffy)

#10 - Rage of Angles (Part 4): Heaven Fire

Glory/Angela: Angels in Hell (Writer: Rob Liefeld)

#1 - Angels in Hell

MaxiMage (Writer: William Messner-Loebs)

#4 - Part 5 - Goin' To Glory

New Man (Writer: Eldon Asp)

#1 - New Day Dawning

Shattered Image (Writers: Kurt Busiek and Barbara Randall Kesel)

#2 - Part 2 of 4

Spawn (Writers as credited)

#9 - Angela (Neil Gaiman)

#28 - Protector (Angela pages written by Neil Gaiman, uncredited)

#30 - The Clan (Todd McFarlane)

#40 - Fugitives, Part 1 (Todd McFarlane)

#43 - Evil (Todd McFarlane)

#46 - Revenge (Todd McFarlane)

#47 - Twisted (Todd McFarlane)

#48 - The System (Todd McFarlane)

#49 - Helter Skelter (Todd McFarlane)

#62 - Return (Todd McFarlane)

#89 - The Devil You Know (Brian Holguin and Todd McFarlane)

#96 - Rules of Engagement (Brian Holguin and Todd McFarlane)

#97 – Heaven's Folly (Brian Holguin and Todd McFarlane)

#98 - The Trouble With Angels (Brian Holguin and Todd McFarlane)

#99 - The Edge of Darkness (Brian Holguin and Todd McFarlane)

#100 - Milestone (Brian Holguin and Todd McFarlane)

#101 - Aftermath (Todd McFarlane)

Spawn Bible (Writers: Andrew Grossberg, Todd McFarlane, Tom Orzechowski and Beau Smith)

#1

Team Youngblood (Writers: Rob Liefeld and Eric Stephenson)

#21 - Rage of Angels Part 3

Youngblood (Writers: Rob Liefeld and Eric Stephenson)

#6 - Rage of Angels Part 2

Once Marvel Comics obtained the character, they didn't waste time inserting her into the Marvel Universe. Her first Marvel appearance came in Age of Ultron - #10 (August 2013), written by Brian Michael Bendis. Since then she has become a mainstay of the Marvel Universe, appearing the pages of the *X-Men*, *Guardians of the Galaxy*, *Thor* and more. None of her Marvel Universe appearances have been written by Neil Gaiman.

Addendum 2: Miracleman at Image

Despite McFarlane's public bluster, he never really attempted to exploit the *Miracleman* character at Image Comics. This might have come about due to McFarlane using the character as bait for Gaiman, and also due to the dubious legal issues around ownership at the time. His first appearance came in *Hellspawn* #6 (February 2001) and his last appearance in the Image Universe came in the *Image Comics* 10th anniversary hardcover edition (December 2005)[1].

McFarlane, who wrote and drew the *Image Comics* entry, drew Miracleman as a figure hiding in the shadows and never clearly seen.

It was intended that *Hellspawn* #13 would introduce the character fully, but this issue was canceled with only a cover existing.

This is a checklist of *Miracleman's* two Image Universe appearances, complete with who wrote the character.

Hellspawn (Writer: Steve Niles)

#6 - The Big Leagues (as Mike Moran)

Image Comics (Writer: Todd McFarlane)

Addendum 3: Miracleman at Marvel

The *Miracleman* series was reprinted by Marvel Comics. Beginning in 2014, they managed to successfully deal with all the diverse creators involved with varying degrees of success and demands.

Alan Moore insisted that his name be removed from the series, this was done, and he was credited as 'The Original Writer'. He also asked that any and all royalties due to him be sent to Mick Anglo.

Marvel couldn't agree fast enough.

"After being initially informed by Neil's lawyer, I had to think about it for a couple of days," Moore said. "I decided that I'm very happy for this book to get published – because this means money will finally go to *Marvelman's* creator, Mick Anglo, and his wife.[1]"

Alan Davis consented to his art being reprinted and provided new covers to the series, as did Garry Leach, Rick Veitch and John Totleben.

Both Davis and Leach were granted a 'Special Thanks' credit in the books.

Marvel had to deal with Dez Skinn as he owns the character *Big Ben.* A license to use the character was achieved quietly and neatly, as was the use of the *Warpsmiths*, which were owned by Garry Leach and Alan Moore.

Artists such as John Romita Jr, Mike Deodato Jr, Neal Adams, Arthur Adams, Bryan Hitch, Gerald Parel, J.G. Jones, Joe Quesada, Alex Ross and many more all contributed variant and regular covers to the series. Todd McFarlane wasn't asked.

Each issue reprinted the original Eclipse comic, plus a plethora of bonus material in the form of scans of original art, sketches, covers and art from the *Warrior* series, text articles, promotional ads and reprints of original Mick Anglo era *Marvelman* stories.

But this time there was no doubt about who owned *Miracleman*. It was, and still is, Marvel Comics.

The reprints received mixed responses. The prices were high ($4.99 per issue) and the bonus content was somewhat hit and miss. Adding to the frustration of some were simple printing errors. Even worse was the censoring of Moore's script, with one word, 'nigger', being blacked out, although it was present in the original series and the Eclipse reprints, and had not caused any fuss at the time. By censoring the word, Marvel merely drew attention to it.

It would appear that Marvel cannot publish anything by Alan Moore without altering it.

Neil Gaiman and Mark Buckingham picked up where they left off. The first series of their trilogy, *The Golden Age*, finally appeared in 2015. The pair then settled down to complete their story. It is scheduled to appear in 2019, but after the series, *The Silver Age*, has been scheduled every year since 2015, the general feeling is that people will believe it when, and if, they finally see it. Next will the final entry in the trilogy, *The Bronze Age*. After that, who knows? At some point *Miracleman* will appear in the Marvel Universe proper.

For those keeping score, *Miracleman's* formal trademark registration number is 4,632,869.

Reading List

As with all good things, there is a reading list that covers some of these topics in far more detail, especially when it comes to the *Miracleman* saga. Most, if not all, of these books are readily available, both in physical and electronic format. Some of these publications I've contributed information and assistance to, both knowingly and unknowingly, but I don't get paid for any sales, so don't think I'm profiting here.

If you got through all of this and want to know more, then I recommend the following:

Prince of Stories: The Many Worlds of Neil Gaiman (St Martin's Press, New York, 2008) by Hank Wagner, Christopher Golden, and Stephen R Bissette. A great book and a brilliant overview of Gaiman's entire career up to 2008. Terrific details on Gaiman's *Miracleman* work.

The Art of Neil Gaiman (Ilex Press, 2014) by Haley Campbell. Written with the direct involvement of Neil Gaiman. If you don't have it, then you should.

Poisoned Chalice: The Extremely Long and Incredibly Complex Story of Marvelman (and Miracleman) (Poisoned Chalice Press, 2018) by Pádraig Ó Méalóid. Cracking good read that covers the history of *Miracleman* and the various incarnations and ownerships. Utterly essential.

The Art of Todd McFarlane: The Devil's in the Details (Image Comics, 2013) by Todd McFarlane. In which McFarlane details his career as he sees it. Great artwork, if you like McFarlane's art.

Kimota! The Miracleman Companion (TwoMorrows Publishing, 2011) by George Khoury. Does it what it says on the box. Excellent overview of *Miracleman* and covers some of the trials and ownership of the character through many, often times contradictory, interviews. Now out of print and an expensive book to find, which is a damned shame.

Image Comics: The Road to Independence (TwoMorrows Publishing, 2007) by George Khoury. Another one that's out of print physically, but available electronically. A good read if you want to know about the formation of Image.

The Comics Journal, in particular issues 95, 165, 172, 174, 185, 237, 241, 248 and 250. All contain great overviews of Eclipse, Image Comics, Neil Gaiman, *Miracleman* and Todd McFarlane.

In addition there's any number of interviews with Alan Moore, Alan Davis, Neil Gaiman, Todd McFarlane, Cat Yronwode and others – including Tony Twist - covering many of the topics raised in this article.

Then there's the legal documents. Deposition, trial transcripts, affidavits, documents and loads, loads more. Feel free to hunt them down. Trust me, it'll cost you an arm and also a leg and there's a lot of legal dross in there that will mean nothing to almost everyone.

I suspect that, towards the end when there were seemingly endless status updates being filed, even the lawyers stopped reading.

Acknowledgements

Special thanks to Chad Eglinton, Pádraig Ó Méalóid, Stephen R Bissette, Paul Neary, Steve Lehmann, Darren Close, Rick Veitch, Gary Chaloner, David DeVries, John Jackson Miller, Maggie Thompson, Glenn Hauman and everyone who has contributed to this project with their comments, remembrances, encouragement and support, especially those who wished to remain anonymous.

Extra special thanks to Todd McFarlane. May you never change, you stubborn, talented fool! You are the gift that keeps on giving.

The author also wishes to thank his family, his wife, Lyndal, and children Kat and Geoffrey, without whose patience, support, encouragement and understanding, I'd never publish anything.

Chapter Notes

McFarlane – Pre-Image

[1] State Press Magazine, 4 Mar 1999
[2] McFarlane Deposition, Mar 1, 2006
[3] State Press Magazine, 4 Mar 1999
[4] McFarlane Deposition, Jun 20, 2002
[5] *Amazing heroes Interviews* #2. 1993
[6] Arizona Republic (Phoenix, Arizona) Aug 15, 2009
[7] State Press Magazine, 4 Mar 1999
[8] *Comic Buyer's Guide* #1271. Apr 3, 1998
[9] Paul Neary, AI, 2006
[10] McFarlane Deposition, Jun 20, 2002

The Amazing Spider-Man

[1] The Amazing Spider-Man, #298–323, 325, 328 (1988–90), written by David Michelinie
[2] Spider-Man #1–14, 16 (1990–91), written by Todd McFarlane
[3] Jim Mooney, a fine penciler and a better inker, was like most of the old-time artists at Marvel at the time who started work in the Golden Age of comics. In Mooney's case, he broke into comics in 1939.
[4] AI with both Esposito and Buscema, 2005
[5] State Press Magazine, 4 Mar 1999
[6] The Gazette (Montreal, Quebec, Canada) Jun 4, 1988
[7] The Ottawa Citizen (Ottawa, Ontario, Canada) Jun 4, 1988
[8] Ditko pencilled and co-plotted the first 38 issues of *Amazing Spider-Man*, plus the origin issue as published in *Amazing Adult Fantasy* #15 and two *Amazing Spider-Man* Annuals
[9] Arizona Republic (Phoenix, Arizona) Mar 23, 1989
[10] *Comics Interview* #81
[11] AI with Marvel Comics Staffer, Dec 2018
[12] AI with Rubinstein, 2005
[13] Robert Kirkman, Vulture, March 2017
[14] Gary Groth, Vulture, March 2017
[15] Ironically some of those artists had broken into the industry years before and had been told to draw like Jack Kirby, John Romita Sr or John Buscema, depending on when they began their careers. Soon they would be told to draw like Rob Liefeld.
[16] *Comics Interview* #133
[17] The Daily Spectrum (Saint George, Utah) Aug 10, 1990
[18] Out of all the writer/artists at Marvel from the 1960s to the 1990s, including Jim Steranko, Jack Kirby, Frank Miller, John Byrne, Walter Simonson, Todd

McFarlane, Erik Larsen, Rob Liefeld and others, it was the much derided Alan Kupperberg who actually produced a book which he wrote, pencilled, inked lettered and coloured. The book was the one-shot *Obnoxio The Clown vs the X-Men*.

[19] *Comics Interview* #81

[20] McFarlane Deposition, Jun 20, 2002

[21] The cover of *Wizard* #1 featured a Spider-Man cover, drawn by McFarlane

[22] The Daily Spectrum (Saint George, Utah) Aug 10, 1990

[23] The Ottawa Citizen (Ottawa, Ontario, Canada) Jun 30, 1990

[24] *Spider-Man* #1, script by Todd McFarlane.

[25] *Amazing Heroes Interviews* #1. Jun 1993

[26] Gaiman Deposition, Jun 24, 2002

[27] AI with Dave deVries, 2018

[28] The Comics Journal #152, August 1992

[29] Arizona Republic (Phoenix, Arizona) Apr 26, 1995

Forming Image

[1] Other inkers in that particular issue were Jim Lee, Scott Williams and Rick Magyar, along with McFarlane himself. Liefeld would also ink McFarlane for a handful of pages in *Spawn* #10 and #11, along with Lee and Marc Silvestri.

[2] Rob Liefeld. Comic Buyer's Guide 1997 Annual

[3] Ibid

[4] Erik Larsen. Comic Buyer's Guide 1997 Annual

[5] McFarlane Deposition, Jun 20, 2002

[6] Jim Valentino. Comic Buyer's Guide 1997 Annual

[7] Ibid

[8] Jim Lee. Comic Buyer's Guide 1997 Annual

[9] Liefeld. Comic Buyer's Guide 1997 Annual

[10] Marc Silvestri. Comic Buyer's Guide 1997 Annual

[11] McFarlane. Comic Buyer's Guide 1997 Annual

[12] Comics Interview #133

[13] Malibu Sun, May 1992

Creating Spawn

[1] Wiater, Stan, and Stephen Bissette. 1993. *Comic book rebels: conversations with the creators of the New Comics*. New York: D.I. Fine.

[2] McFarlane, Motion Hearing, 14 June 2010

[3] Gaiman Deposition, Jun 24, 2002

[4] McFarlane. Comic Buyer's Guide 1997 Annual

[5] Silvestri. Comic Buyer's Guide 1997 Annual

Naming Tony Twist

[1] *Wizard Spawn Tribute*

[2] State Press Magazine, 4 Mar 1999

[3] Ibid
[4] *Comic Buyer's Guide* 1394, Aug 4, 2000
[5] *Spawn* #6, script by Todd McFarlane
[6] *Spawn* #21, script by Todd McFarlane
[7] Cross-examination of Todd McFarlane from first Tony Twist trial

Writing Spawn
[1] *Spawn* #6, script by Todd McFarlane
[2] McFarlane Deposition, Jun 20, 2002
[3] *Amazing Heroes Interviews* #1. Jun 1993
[4] Previews Vol II, #11. Nov 1992
[5] *Amazing Heroes Interviews* #1. Jun 1993
[6] Ibid
[7] Gaiman Deposition, Jun 24, 2002
[8] Comics Interview #119

Creating Angela
[1] Alan Moore would continue to write for Image, and his work featured heavily for McFarlane, Rob Liefeld and Jim Lee's studios and books for the rest of the 1990s, with varying degrees of success (and quality).
[2] The series had originally been under the control of Jim Valentino
[3] Previews Vol II, #11. Nov 1992
[4] Comics Interview #119
[5] Ibid
[6] Gaiman Deposition, Jun 24, 2002
[7] Ibid
[8] Ibid
[9] *Amazing Heroes Interviews* #1. Jun 1993
[10] Wiater, Stan, and Stephen Bissette. 1993. *Comic book rebels: conversations with the creators of the New Comics*. New York: D.I. Fine.
[11] 1963 was a six-issue comic book, written by Alan Moore and illustrated by Stephen Bissette, John Totleben, and Rick Veitch. Dave Gibbons, Don Simpson, and Jim Valentino. The series was to be wrapped up in an Annual but politics around Image Comics at the time (1993) would see the annual never completed. A falling out between Moore and Bissette would see the characters created in 1963 split up, meaning the story will, more than likely, never be published again.
[12] AI with Stephen Bissette, Dec 17, 2018

The Eclipse Saga
[1] Dean Mullaney, *The Comics Journal* #165
[2] Anonymous professional AI, 2018
[3] Alan Davis, *Amazing Heroes* #85, Dec 1985
[4] The San Francisco Examiner (San Francisco, California) Feb 23, 1986

[5] Cat Yronwode, Speakeasy #57
[6] Alan Moore, Interview with Kurt Amacker, September 2009
[7] Ó Méalóid, Pádraig. 2018. Poisoned Chalice: *The Extremely Long and Incredibly Complex Story of Marvelman (and Miracleman)*. Poisoned Chalice Press
[8] Toren Smith, *The Comics Journal* #165
[9] Yronwode, *The Comics Journal* #165
[10] Mullaney, *The Comics Journal* #165
[11] Khoury, George, and Alan Moore. 2010. *Kimota!: the Miracleman companion: the definitive edition*. Raleigh, N.C.: TwoMorrows.
[12] Mullaney to Richard Arndt: http://enjolrasworld.com/richard arndt/web of horror.htm
[13] Campiti, *The Comics Journal* #172
[14] Ibid
[15] Ibid
[16] Khoury, George, and Alan Moore. 2010. *Kimota!: the Miracleman companion: the definitive edition*. Raleigh, N.C.: TwoMorrows.
[17] Campiti, *The Comics Journal* #172
[18] Gaiman, *The Comics Journal* #172
[19] Email from Rick Vieth, April 2019
[20] Khoury, George, and Alan Moore. 2010. *Kimota!: the Miracleman companion: the definitive edition*. Raleigh, N.C.: TwoMorrows.
[21] Ibid
[22] Gaiman, *The Comics Journal* #172
[23] Alan Moore, *The Comics Journal* #172
[24] Yronwode, *Miracleman* #7

Eclipse Auction & Sale
[1] *Comic Buyer's Guide* #1519
[2] Ibid
[3] Ibid
[4] https://www.nolo.com/legal-encyclopedia/bankruptcy/hiding-assets-property-bankruptcy.html
[5] Gaiman Deposition, 24 June, 2002
[6] Terry Fitzgerald Deposition, Jul 23, 2002
[7] McFarlane, *The Comics Journal* #185
[8] Ibid
[9] Letter to Terry Fitzgerald, confirming the sale of Eclipse to Todd McFarlane
[10] McFarlane Deposition, Jun 19, 2002
[11] Gaiman Deposition, Jun 24, 2002
[12] Pádraig Ó Méalóid, http://www.comicsbeat.com/poisoned-chalice-part-11-the-twilight-of-eclipse/
[13] Cat Yronwode, http://www.comicsbeat.com/poisoned-chalice-part-11-the-twilight-of-eclipse/

[14] John Jackson Miller, Facebook post, 19 November 2018
[15] https://www.copyright.gov/help/faq/faq-general.html#automatic
[16] https://www.copyright.gov/circs/circ01.pdf
[17] The San Francisco Examiner (San Francisco, California) Feb 23, 1986
[18] Marvels and Miracles LLC Proof of Claim, Jan 16, 2006
[19] Agreement between Eclipse Enterprises and Quality Communications, Feb 7, 1985

Todd vs Rob: Image Implodes
[1] Larry Marder Deposition, 19 June 2002
[2] Marder. Comic Buyer's Guide 1997 Annual
[3] *The Comics Journal* #225, July 2000
[4] Ibid
[5] Top Cow was the name of Silvestri's studio
[6] Silvestri. Comic Buyer's Guide 1997 Annual
[7] State Press Magazine, 4 Mar 1999
[8] Scripting a book means that the writer puts the words into the story that another writer has written.
[9] CompuServe message boards, 3 Sept 1996
[10] Ibid
[11] *The Comics Journal* #195, April 1997
[12] Resignation letter, Rob Liefeld, 4 Sept 1996
[13] *The Comics Journal* #190, Sept 1996
[14] Liefeld. Comic Buyer's Guide 1997 Annual
[15] Actually, he was. Marc Silvestri had chosen to take his Top Cow Studios titles away from Image but had not resigned from the board of Image Comics. The fact that Liefeld did not contact Silvestri shows the level of animosity between the two at the time.
[16] *The Comics Journal* #195, April 1997
[17] Ibid
[18] Ibid
[19] Ibid
[20] AI with Erik Larson, 2008
[21] Wizard Magazine #77, January 1998

Tony Twist Sues
[1] *Wizard*, April 1996
[2] *Wizard Spawn Tribute*. The same issue of Wizard featured another admission of naming, "Johnny and Peter. Real-life Persona: John Byrne and Peter David. Relation: Close friends and synchronized swimming partners (um, actually McFarlane has been feuding with these guys for quite some time.) These two, McFarlane says with a bit of sarcasm, are named for his two 'good pals' John Byrne and Peter David. McFarlane takes shots at them at any time he can, and this is one of those times where he can."

[3] Cross-examination of Todd McFarlane from first Tony Twist trial
[4] Hockey Hall of Fame entry
[5] St. Louis Post-Dispatch (St. Louis, Missouri) Jul 7, 2000
[6] Calgary Herald (Calgary, Alberta, Canada) Jul 8, 2000
[7] Riverfront Times, October 2006
[8] St. Louis Post-Dispatch (St. Louis, Missouri) Jul 6, 2000
[9] Edmonton Journal (Edmonton, Alberta, Canada) Jul 7, 2000
[10] The Devil You Know...: An interview with Todd McFarlane
[11] Time Magazine, Aug 8, 2007
[12] Marder Deposition, Jun 19, 2002

Todd McFarlane Runs Neil Gaiman Around
[1] McFarlane. The Devil You Know...An interview with Todd McFarlane
[2] Gaiman Deposition, Jun 24, 2002
[3] McFarlane Deposition, Jun 19, 2002
[4] Gaiman Deposition, Jun 24, 2002
[5] Marder Deposition, Jun 19, 2002
[6] Letter from Gaiman to McFarlane, July 1997
[7] Gaiman testimony, Angela trial
[8] Ibid
[9] McFarlane Deposition, Jun 19, 2002
[10] Gaiman Deposition, Jun 24, 2002
[11] Marder, Tony Twist Trial, 2005

The Miracleman Trademark
[1] The Applicant was Todd McFarlane Productions
[2] The Opposer was Marvels & Miracles, LLC.
[3] Gaiman, The Comics Journal #237

First Gaiman Trial
[1] Gaiman, Wisconsin State Journal, Oct 2, 2002
[2] McFarlane testimony, Angela Trial
[3] Jury verdict, Oct 3, 2002
[4] Gaiman Deposition, Jun 24, 2002
[5] Neil Gaiman's Journal: Last Legal Post for a long time
[6] Dave Sim, letter to Erik Larsen, Jul 27, 2005
[7] Erik Larsen, quoted on Comics Alliance, Aug 3, 2010

Let's Twist Again
[1] Tony Twist, Riverfront Times, October 2006
[2] Hanover to McFarlane, May 24, 2004
[3] Cross-examination of Todd McFarlane
[4] McFarlane. The Devil You Know...: An interview with Todd McFarlane

Todd McFarlane Productions

[1] Alan Inglis Deposition, Aug 22, 2002
[2] McFarlane Deposition, Jun 2, 2002
[3] McFarlane Deposition, Jun 20, 2002
[4] Inglis Deposition, Mar 31, 2006
[5] Inglis Deposition Aug 22, 2002
[6] McFarlane Deposition, Jun 20, 2002
[7] Ibid
[8] Inglis Deposition, Mar 31, 2006
[9] McFarlane Deposition, Jun 20, 2002
[10] Ibid
[11] Ibid
[12] Ibid
[13] Ibid
[14] Inglis Deposition, Mar 31, 2006
[15] Ibid

Settlements

[1] The bonuses payable to McFarlane were $7,500 for any TV special and $5,000 for any half hour show shown on TV

Gaiman Wins A Miracle(man)

[1] McFarlane Deposition, Jul 20, 2002
[2] McFarlane, *Haunted by Comics* Interview, September 2009
[3] Holguin's testimony, Jun 14, 2006
[4] Ibid
[5] McFarlane's testimony, Jun 14, 2006
[6] The clause, 'with prejudice', now meant that Gaiman gave up any and all rights to pursue his claim in any future suit against McFarlane involving the same characters
[7] Final Judgment, 3 February 2012
[8] McFarlane, Newsarama, Mar 25, 2013

McFarlane On The Offensive

[1] Advertisement for *The Art of Being Spawn*, 2012
[2] Simmons, Al, (2012) *The Art of Being Spawn*, Scottsdale Media. AZ, unpublished
[3] McFarlane's editor on his Spider-Man run. Despite displaying a hostile attitude towards writers and editors, McFarlane has often credited Salicrup as being the best editor he'd had.
[4] Simmons, Al, (2012) *The Art of Being Spawn*, Scottsdale Media. AZ, unpublished
[5] *Captain America* 117, Sept 1969. An earlier black super hero, *The Black Panther*, was introduced by Lee and Jack Kirby (*The Fantastic Four* #56, July

1966), but the Panther's alter-ego was from a fictional African country named Wakanda.

[6] Ibid

[7] Verified Complaint, McFarlane v Simmons

[8] It isn't known if the book was actually available to the general public.

In The End

[1] *Amazing Heroes Interviews* #2. 1993

And Then

[1] Westfield Comics Blog: Todd McFarlane on Image's Spawn #200. 4 January, 2010

[2] McFarlane, Vulture, March 2017

Miracleman at Image

[1] In an ironic move, the Image 10th Anniversary book was announced in 2001 and solicited to appear in February 2002. It finally made it to stores in late December 2005. As with *Image United*, those involved – in this case Erik Larsen, Marc Silvestri, Jim Valentino and Todd McFarlane – blamed one another for the delay at various times.

Reading List

[1] Moore, www.mania.com

Printed in Dunstable, United Kingdom

76959389R00119